CW00421592

London's New Routemaster

London's New Routemaster

Tony Lewin

Foreword by
Thomas Heatherwick

MERRELL
LONDON · NEW YORK

Published in association with

**TRANSPORT
FOR LONDON**

Designed for Londoners

Introducing London's latest landmark,
the new bus for London.
Find out more at tfl.gov.uk/buses

Newer. Sleeker. Better.

MAYOR OF LONDON

 CLEANER AIR FOR **LONDON**

Transport for London

MAR 0140.12.11

Foreword

In 2008, when I was campaigning to be elected mayor of the greatest city on Earth, I made a pledge to Londoners: to rid the streets of the dangerous and ineffective 'bendy bus', and to replace it with a modern-day Routemaster that would stand as an icon of London.

I have very fond memories of the redoubtable Routemaster, a remarkable vehicle whose design and brilliant engineering enabled it to serve London and Londoners for a remarkable fifty years. I was as bereft as anyone when these beloved vehicles, so synonymous with our capital city, were put out to pasture. That's why I am so proud of the fact that we now have a new Routemaster on the streets of London – one of the cleanest, greenest buses around. It's already running on routes 9, 11, 24, 148 and 390, with a handful on route 38 as well.

I've been fascinated by every stage of the New Routemaster's creation, from the design phase to witnessing the life-size static mock-up – which staggered me when I first saw it – to the sight of these beautiful buses slipping serenely off the production line and on to London's streets.

Conceived by Thomas Heatherwick, the magician who brought us the Olympic Cauldron, the New Routemaster is a masterpiece of design. It is also driving employment throughout the United Kingdom. It's supporting hundreds of jobs at Wrightbus in Northern Ireland, where the bus is manufactured. Then there are the engines from Darlington, the seats from Telford, the seat moquette from Huddersfield, the ramps from Hoddesdon, the Treadmaster flooring from Liskeard and the destination signs from Middleton, just outside Manchester. It is the embodiment of a point I often make: that investment in London helps to boost the rest of the UK economy, directly and indirectly.

When I went to Ballymena, and saw dozens of the buses being made in the new Wrightbus plant, I felt a sense of awe and the certainty that this was the most wonderful project I had ever been involved in. Soon, all 600 of the original production order will be in service, operating across twenty routes and delivering huge benefits to passengers, to air quality and to the international prestige of the capital.

As you travel around London, take a look at this feat of British engineering – at the noble curve of its brow, like a bowler hat or an African elephant – in its natural habitat. I firmly believe that the New Routemaster will become just as iconic as its forebear, if not more so. I have no doubt that the legions of tourists who visit us each year won't be able to walk past the bus without taking a photo for their album or a 'selfie' to tweet to their friends. Above all, this bus says much about the optimism and dynamism of this city, and of its people.

Boris Johnson

Boris Johnson served as Conservative MP for Henley-on-Thames between 2001 and 2008. Since being elected Mayor of London in May 2008, he has overseen the introduction of a hugely popular cycle-hire scheme and the New Routemaster, the cleanest and greenest diesel hybrid in the world.

Foreword

In 2001 I was asked by a British television programme to argue for a piece of design that I believed to be important to the United Kingdom. I had no hesitation in choosing the original Routemaster, and suggested that London buses should be seen not only as pieces of industrial design, but also as two-storey buildings on wheels that need to be thought of and cared for as part of the capital's architecture.

In the following years, my studio team and I became increasingly interested in the collective experience of cities. When the 'New Bus for London' project was initiated by Transport for London and the Mayor, we saw an opportunity to make a meaningful difference to the lives of millions of Londoners.

Our work was inspired by the legacy of Frank Pick, who, in the first half of the last century, drove the design ethos not only of London Transport but also of the wider industrial community. He envisaged a public transportation system that didn't just get you to where you wanted to go, but added to the cultural life of the city along the way.

In the decades that followed Pick's tenure at London Transport, an accumulation of health and safety regulations and the loss of a wider design vision had a big impact on London's buses and, in particular, passenger experience. We had a bus system that moved people around, but which had forgotten to consider how it made people feel.

Having been lucky enough to be chosen to lead the design of the New Routemaster, we were faced with many practical considerations. Throughout the process, however, we attempted to remain focused on the human experience of the passenger and the architectural experience of the bus within the city. This was a great opportunity not only to meet all the statutory regulations, and even to be 40 per cent more efficient, but also, crucially, to champion the dignity of the passenger.

The outcome of our collaboration with TfL and bus manufacturer Wrightbus was a design that tries to create a better balance between infrastructural need and the human experience of bus travel in the capital.

Thomas Heatherwick

Thomas Heatherwick is a world-renowned designer and the founder of Heatherwick Studio. Based in London, the studio is notable for its award-winning work in architecture, urban infrastructure, sculpture, design and strategic thinking.

Preface

The New Routemaster, as it has become known, certainly had a lot to live up to, given its famous and much-loved predecessor. In my view, it has surpassed all expectations. As a result of a bold and ambitious decision by the Mayor, London now has a new bus that is visually stunning, operationally efficient and fit for the challenges of a rapidly growing twenty-first-century city.

In the words of Frank Pick, the first chief executive of London Transport, 'everyday things should be not only functional, but pleasing to the eye'. The New Routemaster delivers entirely on that score. People stop dead in their tracks when they see one of these magnificent vehicles for the first time.

There is, of course, so much more to this bus than just good looks. It has been designed from scratch to ensure that it meets the needs not only of our passengers but also of the operating conditions of London. We also recognised the absolute necessity of significantly reducing engine emissions as part of improving London's air quality. The New Routemaster might be red on the outside, but its beating heart is green. Using the latest hybrid technology, it has set a benchmark for the industry in this area.

In a country in which making things is sometimes regarded as a lost art, this whole process has also reminded us of just how agile and innovative our designers and manufacturers actually are.

One of the most incredible aspects of this vehicle is the breathtaking speed with which it has come about – from drawing board to entering passenger service in just over two years. That is simply astonishing, and reflects the extremely successful partnership between Heatherwick Studio in London and the highly respected Ballymena-based manufacturer Wrightbus. Their work together has been inspirational.

Transport for London's purpose is to keep our city working and growing, and to make life here better. I am proud that we have been able to work with a range of such talented partners to create a beautiful new bus to help us do just that.

Sir Peter Hendy, CBE

Sir Peter Hendy was appointed Commissioner of Transport for London in 2006, having previously served as the organisation's Managing Director of Surface Transport. He led, and played a key role in preparing for, the successful operation of London's transport network during the 2012 Olympic and Paralympic Games.

Introduction

In London, buses make a real difference to the way we live, how we get about and the manner in which this remarkable city operates. They provide a vital service for millions of people, linking homes to jobs, schools and hospitals in every part of the capital, with the vast majority of Londoners never more than 400 metres (1,300 feet) from a bus stop.

Buses are the workhorses of the capital's public-transport network, and carry more passengers every year than all the other buses in England combined. More people are travelling on our buses than at any time since the 1960s, and customer satisfaction is at an all-time high.

London's bus network is one of the largest in the world, and is fully accessible, providing an invaluable lifeline to many disabled and older passengers. Our 8,700-strong bus fleet serves 19,500 bus stops across 700 routes. London buses operate 24 hours a day, 364 days of the year, supporting the needs of our growing city and, in turn, helping London to function as the engine room of the UK's economy.

Our buses, the pulsing red arteries of the capital, make possible the movement of large numbers of people around the city – across the centre and to the extremities. While most of us sleep, the legions of people who prepare the city for the following day rely on our night buses. Almost half of those who travel on our 24-hour routes are going to, or from, work.

London Transport stopped designing its own buses more than forty years ago. In the intervening period, bus types have come and gone. Now, in the twenty-first century, the requirements for a London bus are quite different from those for buses operating elsewhere in the country: multiple doors for open and fast boarding, very low emissions for air quality, and an iconic design suitable for a city of international repute. The New Routemaster has thus restarted a tradition of carefully designed vehicles for London – leading the way, as is entirely right, in our world-class capital city.

Leon Daniels

Leon Daniels was appointed as Transport for London's Managing Director of Surface Transport in 2011. He is responsible for a broad range of sustainable transport and an annual budget of more than £2.5 billion. During 2012 he successfully managed and delivered the roads and surface-transport elements of the London Olympics – the first 'public transport' Games.

1

The Background

What is big, red and moves the equivalent of the entire population of Scotland every day of the week? Which national treasure is so imprinted on our consciousness that we measure the height of our buildings by it and compare the weight of whales to it? And why does such sentimentality still cling to the double-ding of a bell, the grinding of gears on a hill and the faint whiff of exhaust fumes when stepping back on to the street?

The answer, of course, is the London bus, and more specifically the double-decker and its most famous incarnation, the Routemaster. For reasons that perhaps only a social psychologist could decode, an incurable romance continues to surround these formidable movers of people and possessions: blazers, shiny black shoes and satchels on the journey to school; teenage high jinks on the way back from the cinema; peering through the steamed-up windows of the top deck as the sights of wintry London swirl past. For all but the very youngest among us, these are formative experiences, the stuff of poetic musings and of a familiar and homely environment that allowed us to explore away from home in safety.

But now, with today's generation of super-efficient, climate-controlled and automated buses, there is a widespread feeling that that romance has evaporated: the electronic beep of an Oyster-card reader is no substitute for the witty comments of a chatty conductor, let alone the click-click-whirr of his ticket machine, while the dehumanising, hospital-like glare of the sterile interior is an invitation to shut off, rather than socialise.

London's 8,600 buses carry a remarkable 2.3 billion passengers a year on some 700 separate routes; indeed, more than half of all bus journeys in England are in London, and bus travel in the capital is booming. Yet, somehow, the technology that enables these advances is coming to signify anonymity and alienation, wrenching the bus network away from its roots as a sensibly social and egalitarian means of getting around. Our sociologist might suggest that the emotional bond between man and bus is under strain, threatening to turn bus travel into nothing more than a commodity.

Pages 14–15
A congested Queen Victoria Street, looking west, in 1920s London. A wide variety of vehicles can be seen, including B-Type, K-Type and NS-Type buses, taxis, private cars and horse-drawn delivery vehicles.

Right
Source of inspiration … The highly successful Routemaster became a national – and international – treasure during its four decades of London service. Several examples still operate on Heritage routes.

But all need not be lost. With the stylishly shaped New Routemaster and its warm, welcoming interior and customer-friendly conductor – not to mention its super-clean hybrid propulsion – the bus is working its way back into passengers' affections, and bus travel is once again on the agenda as a quality experience for all.

It All Began with a Promise

'London needs a fresh perspective', declared Boris Johnson in *Getting Londoners Moving*, the transport manifesto for his 2008 mayoral election campaign. 'I want to introduce a 21st century Routemaster that will once again give London an iconic bus that Londoners can be proud of … I want to see the next generation Routemaster, with conductors, running on the streets of London by the end of my first term as Mayor.'

The manifesto then explained in broad terms how the '21st century Routemaster' would gradually be phased in to replace the so-called bendy buses, which, Johnson declared, should be scrapped (as it turned out, the last of the bendy buses would be withdrawn a matter of weeks before the first New Routemaster hit London's streets). What was lacking was any detail on precisely what sort of bus could serve as a reincarnated Routemaster; instead, the prospective mayor skilfully tempted voters with the enticing prospect of an open competition to design a renewed Routemaster. Time and again, the manifesto describes the proposed new bus as 'iconic' and 'emblematic of our great city'.

Yet the preceding eight years under Ken Livingstone's Labour administration had seen investment in buses rise significantly and bus use nearly double since its low point in 1982. To all intents and purposes, public transport was thriving, and London buses already appeared to be on a roll – so why did the manifesto pledge to introduce another new bus prove to be such a vote winner?

Whipped up by a willing media, the backlash against the bendy buses was already in full swing by the summer of 2007, with Livingstone implicitly blamed for having withdrawn the old Routemasters to make

'My vision is a London with trains and buses that can compete with the very best in the world – for speed, reliability, quality of journey and basic aesthetics.'

Getting Londoners Moving
Boris Johnson

'I want to introduce a 21st century Routemaster that will once again give London an iconic bus that Londoners can be proud of and I will renew it for the next generation.'

Getting Londoners Moving
Boris Johnson

way for what were disparagingly described as articulated monsters. It was in September that year, as reported in the *Evening Standard*, that Johnson fired his first well-aimed but somewhat overstated salvo in what would become the war of the buses, declaring that if he were elected mayor, 'we should on day one, act one, scene one, hold a competition to get rid of the bendy bus … It's not beyond the wit of man to design a new Routemaster that will stand as an icon of this city.'

While Johnson's political opponents appeared to take the reincarnated Routemaster proposal as a sign of the folly of his campaign, the idea began to gain traction in the most surprising quarters. Even the hardened petrolheads at *Autocar* magazine were inspired to commission a respected design firm, Capoco, to come up with a proposal for just such a bus. The result, published in December 2007 and delivered to Johnson's campaign headquarters by *Autocar*'s associate editor, Hilton Holloway, is credited by some with giving the revived Routemaster idea the credibility it needed. Holloway recalls one politician declaring that the magazine's cutaway drawing 'had changed the debate completely because it was now clear that the aspiring mayor's vision was viable'.

Political considerations aside, one possible explanation for the resonance of the 'new Routemaster' message could be that public transport has always been seen as being dear to London's heart, an integral part of its identity as a city. Somewhere along the line it seems that, despite the new-found efficiency and cleanliness of the spruced-up bus and Tube networks, this identity and affection had come unstuck. And nowhere was this clearer than in the case of the buses: while every major international city had its own underground system, and while London's black-cab taxis were as unique as ever, there was now very little to distinguish London's buses from those plying the streets of almost any other large conurbation in the United Kingdom.

'I want to see the next generation Routemaster, with conductors, running on the streets of London by the end of my first term as Mayor.'

Getting Londoners Moving
Boris Johnson

Boris Johnson's manifesto for the 2008 London mayoral election committed his administration to introducing a worthy successor to the Routemaster. It proved a powerful vote winner.

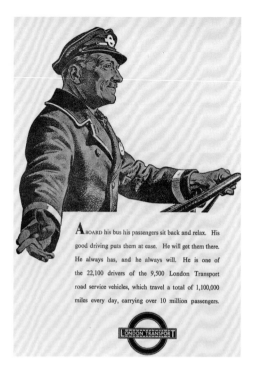

A<small>BOARD</small> his bus his passengers sit back and relax. His good driving puts them at ease. He will get them there. He always has, and he always will. He is one of the 22,100 drivers of the 9,500 London Transport road service vehicles, which travel a total of 1,100,000 miles every day, carrying over 10 million passengers.

LONDON TRANSPORT

A London Transport poster from the bus boom years blends customer reassurance with impressive corporate statistics and the portrayal of the driver as a role model to promote recruitment.

That went against the grain for Johnson and his mission to become the guardian of London's global image.

The distinctive Routemaster, that very visible symbol of London given worldwide celebrity through film, television and a massive merchandising industry, had been traded in for a series of anonymous, off-the-shelf models whose square-rigged shapes could have been shipped in from Chicago or Shanghai, Berlin or Bogota. In short, the emotional connection between the public and the bus had been severed: the friendly face and warm heart had been sacrificed in the name of clinical efficiency and lurid furnishings.

The mention of bringing back conductors was a further reminder of how that personal, human touch had been lost. Among other things, the conductor symbolised an earlier, more secure time when help and advice were always on hand. And nothing was more alien or impersonal than the bendy bus, on which passengers could be as much as 18 metres (60 feet) away from the driver, with as many as 140 fellow passengers in between. The future mayor saw this as an issue of great importance to the travelling public. But to understand why this resonated so strongly right across the capital, a short history lesson might be in order.

Buses, People and Politics

Londoners have always enjoyed a personal and almost possessive relationship with their public transport system. They may love it or loathe it, but few remain indifferent to it; and, perhaps for this reason, transport in London is invariably a political talking point and thus rarely out of the headlines.

In the many changes of name, organisation, operation, ownership and control over its eleven-decade existence, London's bus network

London Transport has always been highly conscious of its image, regularly issuing publicity photographs of passengers, vehicles and crew. Featured here are some of the early pay-on-entry buses, including the unsuccessful experiment with turnstiles (second column, third row down).

London's buses have always transported almost twice as many passengers per day as the Underground network, with queuing arrangements gradually becoming more civilised. With progressive design always featuring in London Transport's activities, many of its bus shelters and other facilities were designed by such prominent architects as Charles Holden.

has seen its fortunes ebb and flow with some regularity, sometimes boosted by the economic climate, and at other times dragged down by it. Equally, strong central control has frequently led to good times for the bus system, while on other occasions it has held back progress.

After the unregulated competition of the 1920s gave way to the newly formed London Transport (officially, the London Passenger Transport Board) in 1933, investment – backed by government guarantees – became more systematic, bus types became more standardised and bus use climbed steadily. Nationalised by the Labour government in 1948, London Transport pressed ahead with the development of such advanced buses as the RT and the Routemaster. Cars were in short supply, having been declared an export priority, and between the late 1940s and early 1950s this led to bus travel enjoying a few boom years, hampered only by chronic staff shortages. Indeed, according to current senior transport executives, it was only through active recruitment of new staff from the Commonwealth that London Transport was able to maintain its services throughout the 1950s.

Responsibility for London Transport and London's buses was formally handed over to the Greater London Council in 1970, but important changes had been in the offing since 1968. The most far-reaching of these was the move towards driver-only operation, something that threatened the whole concept of double-deckers and, at one point, had London Transport planning to overhaul the entire network and use predominantly single-deckers. While the changes of 1970 resulted in the organisation losing the power to design and build its own buses (a measure designed to protect the already struggling Leyland group), further upheaval came in 1984, with the Conservative government preparing London's bus operations for the introduction of competitive tendering and eventual privatisation. Bus-passenger numbers had been on the wane for some years, as car ownership (which quadrupled in London between 1950 and 1970) soared, and bus travel

The *Big Red Book* is issued to all London bus drivers, and provides guidance on everything from wheelchair access to public-announcement etiquette.

had become stigmatised as a poor person's alternative; furthermore, declining revenues meant that few new buses could be ordered, and the fleet was ageing. Although, in contrast to the rest of the country, London's bus operations were never actually deregulated, London Transport's role was reduced to that of an arm's-length supervising body, allocating route franchises to newly independent operators, which were responsible for their own fleets and staff. By the beginning of 1995, all of these operators were in private hands, either as a result of management and employee buy-outs, or through purchase by large national operators; this led to the spectacle of a huge and confusing variety of colours and liveries, further diluting the traditional image of the red London bus.

The shift in the industry's structure would have significant consequences as far as bus design and production were concerned. No longer was there the critical mass of demand to justify a dedicated new design shaped around London's particular needs; no longer could specialised bus manufacturers survive purely on the strength of orders for London. Yet the need for new buses had now become pressing: driver-only operation was required to save on staff costs, low-floor entrances were needed for compliance with upcoming disability legislation, and emissions restrictions were looming. The familiar Routemaster failed on all three counts, and the cash-conscious operators, committed to their franchises, were forced to shop around for off-the-peg models to replace it. In the words of one executive working in the industry at the time, it was a mad rush to buy 'anything and everything'.

These uninspiring and anonymous buses would serve only to prolong the malaise of London's surface transport, a situation that continued until the formation of Transport for London (TfL) in 2000, part of the Greater London Authority and under the control of the mayor of London. Investment in public transport, including buses, rose significantly during Ken Livingstone's two terms as

mayor. Yet even under TfL, the bus operators remained independent and sourced their buses on the international market.

In marked contrast to earlier decades, London's bus service was now improving and passenger numbers were on the rise. What was conspicuous by its absence, however, was a centralised purchasing policy. This led to a wide variety of bus types, not all of them best suited to London's conditions or Londoners' preferences. The much-discussed bendy bus — in actual fact a Mercedes-Benz Citaro — was a case in point: although it ticked all the technical boxes as a cost-effective and convenient driver-only bus, it failed to connect emotionally with its users. The operators loved it but politically it was unloved, engendering none of the popular affection enjoyed by the older buses. And it was precisely this that Johnson sought to put right when, following his successful election campaign, he entered the mayor's office in May 2008.

At the end of his first four-year term, Johnson had made good on what to some had seemed like an impossible promise. First, the bendy bus had gone — dismissed by Johnson, when questioned for this book, as 'a jack-knifed diplodocus which got stuck around corners, gave fare dodgers a joyful ride and was not fit for our fine city' — and, secondly, a clutch of shiny neo-Routemasters had entered service, in time for the London Olympics. By this stage, the bus had been given its official designation, LT, chosen on the spur of the moment by Sir Peter Hendy, Commissioner of Transport for London, and Leon Daniels, Managing Director for Surface Transport, while on a visit to the Wrightbus factory in Northern Ireland. 'It felt right as a nod to the old organisation, London Transport,' explains Daniels, 'and it was also an acknowledgement of the design cues, such as the rear platform and stairs, taken from the original Routemaster, designed by London Transport.' And now the New Routemaster has become the latest in a long line of buses that for more than a century have come to define London and make their mark — sometimes good, sometimes bad — on the capital.

Bendy buses were efficient, but were seen as easy targets by fare dodgers. At 18 metres long, they proved unpopular with other Londoners, especially cyclists.

Buses in London: The Evolution of an Icon

Right
Horses continued to provide the motive power for London's buses well into the twentieth century, but disappeared quickly when motor-driven buses appeared.

Above, far right
The X-Type, the first London bus designed especially for use in the capital, employed the latest technology. Just sixty were built.

Horse-drawn double-deckers 1880s

Almost 4,000 horse-drawn buses were in service in London by the end of the nineteenth century; the first double-deckers had appeared around 1880. Electric trams arrived in 1901, and 1904 marked the start of the first regular motor-powered bus service: Thomas Tilling's route from Peckham to Oxford Circus. Buses were run by a wide variety of competing operators, including the London General Omnibus Company (LGOC), founded by a French entrepreneur. The smaller operators would later coalesce around LGOC and eventually form London Transport.

X-Type 1909

The first bus specially designed for London, and emanating from AEC's works in Walthamstow, the X-Type drew together ideas from the best contemporary bus designs. The driver sat behind the engine and above the chassis; seating was for sixteen, facing sideways, in the lower saloon, with eighteen on the upper deck, accessed via stairs at the back. Metropolitan Police regulations still ruled out an enclosed roof for upper-deck passengers (on the grounds of stability), while the gearbox used chains instead of gears, the latter being considered by the police to be too noisy.

B-Type 1910

Building on experience gained from the X-Type, LGOC's chief engineer Frank Searle soon came up with the much-improved B-Type, which would cement his reputation as the father of the reliable motor bus. The B-Type itself was an immediate success, demonstrating the advantages of standardisation in manufacture and routine maintenance; indeed, its reliability enabled LGOC to open up new and longer routes around the capital. With similar carrying capacity to its predecessor, the B-Type gained headlights in 1913, enabling it to provide the first night-time route, and famously saw service on the western front during the First World War.

K-Type 1919

Developed by LGOC immediately after the war, the K-Type represented a further step forward for bus design. By placing the driver alongside the engine, rather than behind it, the K-Type gained longer passenger compartments within the same overall length, starting a trend that lasted until the arrival of rear-engined buses in the 1960s. Wider bodywork allowed the seating to be rearranged, too, the new paired forward-facing seats giving a total capacity of forty-six. The K-Type's wheels were still solid-tyred, however: pneumatic tyres became standard across London buses only in the late 1920s.

Far left
An evolution of the X-Type, the B-Type is the most famous of the early buses. It also became the first standard bus type to be deployed across the whole of London.

Above
The K-Type broke with truck tradition and placed the driver alongside the engine, setting a pattern for future bus design.

This poster from 1947 is typical of London Transport's high standards of presentation. The large number of buses in use at that time, as indicated by the statistics, recall an age before mass car ownership.

Right
The NS-Type marked a further advance, with a lower chassis giving more space, easier access and improved stability.

Above, far right
The three-axle layout of the elegant 1929 LT enabled it to carry more passengers – an important consideration when competing against trolleybuses and trams.

NS-Type 1923

Another big step forward in bus design, the NS-Type remained in service until the late 1930s. With its upholstered seats, it was much more comfortable than earlier buses, which had been fitted with wooden benches. The greatest advance, however, was in the chassis: this now sat lower than the axles, rather than being perched above them, resulting in a lower floor height and much easier passenger access on to the rear deck. A secondary and much-needed benefit was a lower centre of gravity and improved stability; even so, the Metropolitan Police still refused to allow the NS-Type a roof for the upper deck. Later, it gained both a roof and pneumatic tyres, illustrating the rapid progress being made in bus design.

LT 1929

Closely related to the ST series (see below), the LT was notable for two main reasons: its three-axle layout, enabling it to carry a greater number of passengers, and its innovative use of a powerful six-cylinder petrol engine linked to a four-speed gearbox. By this time the Associated Equipment Company, in effect LGOC's in-house bus designer and manufacturer, had moved to a larger site in Southall, and, with smooth-riding pneumatic tyres and enclosed upper decks in use, the London bus fleet was regularly carrying more passengers than either the tram network or the underground system.

AT YOUR SERVICE

One of the 22,000 drivers of the 9,500 London Transport road service vehicles which travel a total of 1,100,000 miles every day, carrying more than ten million passengers.

Right
The ST family was produced with a variety of body styles, eventually gaining a modern fully enclosed cab and a full-length upper deck.

Above, far right
Trolleybuses were a common sight on many London streets. They were efficient but often cumbersome in operation.

ST 1929
STL 1932

With the ST, the double-decker bus began to approach its definitive form. As with the LT, a court case between LGOC and the Metropolitan Police had allowed the ST's full-length upper deck to gain a roof; in addition, the tyres were now pneumatic, the driver's cab became partially enclosed and the rear stairs fully enclosed. This established a template that would remain familiar for half a century, culminating in the 1960s with the Routemaster. The longer STL upped the stakes again, with a modern-looking full-length upper deck fully enclosing the driver's cab. The STL seated sixty, and was also among the first buses to move to diesel power.

K2 trolleybus 1938

Introduced throughout the 1930s to replace the rail-bound tram system, London's trolleybuses remained in service on some routes until the early 1960s, when they were finally replaced by RTs and Routemasters. With their three-axle layout they were able to carry more weight and passengers (seventy in total) than the diesel buses they competed with, and they offered the advantage of smooth and near-silent operation; on busy routes they proved more efficient than conventional types of bus. Some 1,800 saw service, most built to a similar template, with an open rear platform and full-length upper and lower decks. The 1938 K2 pictured above was one of the later types.

RT 1939

Designed just before the Second World War but delayed in its production, the RT was the first of London Transport's iconic bus designs, setting the standard for future buses and demonstrating the wisdom of the organisation's policy of standardisation and streamlined maintenance. Huge numbers entered service, making the 1950s the heyday of the bus as trams and, later, trolleybuses were finally replaced; in 1952, for instance, London buses carried 8 million people a day. Drivers appreciated the RT for its easy, air-assisted gear change and brakes, while the smooth exterior style and high-quality, easily cleaned interior helped make the RT a hit with commuters and tourists alike.

Routemaster (RM) 1959

The first truly modern bus, and widely celebrated as a design classic, the Routemaster replaced not only London's remaining trolleybuses but also the RT. The Routemaster was revolutionary in so many ways: its construction, inspired by wartime aircraft manufacture, was a lightweight unitary aluminium framework rather than a separate steel chassis and body; its controls were power-operated, making it light to drive; and its greater width and length meant it could seat sixty-four passengers. It was durable, fuel efficient, comfortable and attractive, all of which kept it in service for a remarkable four decades and helped to make it a powerful symbol of London.

Far left
The RT benefited from an advanced but systematic design, paving the way for the Routemaster, also shaped by London Transport's Bill Durrant. The RT's roll-out was delayed by the Second World War.

Above
The Routemaster set a style that has never dated, but its construction and engineering marked major advances, too.

Right and far right
Bus design experienced
something of a crisis
in the 1970s, as driver-
only operation forced
the fleet towards
rear-engined buses that
were often unreliable in
service, and which lacked
the personality of the
Routemaster. Examples
include the Daimler
Fleetline and Leyland
Titan.

Daimler Fleetline 1971

If the 1940s and early 1950s were the boom
years for London's buses, the decades that
followed saw a sharp decline in both their
popularity and the quality of the service
they provided. Growing car ownership was
shrinking the demand for inner-city bus travel,
and the need to reduce operating costs had
forced London Transport not only to promote
driver-only buses but also to contemplate a
near-wholesale move to single-deckers. The
rear-entrance Routemaster, with its two-
person crew, was no longer the right bus for
the moment. London Transport was now
unable to commission its own buses, so from
the early 1970s a succession of off-the-shelf
rear-engined double-deckers, with the driver –
or a troublesome turnstile – taking the fares,
began to appear. These buses were unloved
and often unreliable, and dragged down the
image of bus travel.

Leyland Titan 1978

Leyland, whose constituent companies
included many of the famous names of the UK
bus industry, collaborated closely with London
Transport to develop the Titan, seeking to
correct the mistakes of the first generation
of rear-engined, front-entrance driver-only
double-deckers. Industrial strife plagued
much of its manufacturing history, but more
than a thousand eventually entered London
service. As in the case of the Daimler Fleetline
(left) and the MCW Metrobus (opposite),
early models featured coin-operated entry
turnstiles; however, these proved unpopular
and, more significantly, unreliable in service,
and were later removed in favour of extra
seating. The Titan was at least reliable,
with many remaining in operation into the
new millennium.

2000 ▶	2002 ▶	2005 ▶	2007 ▶	2008
TfL formed as part of new Greater London Authority	First bendy buses enter service	Last standard services for original Routemaster	September **London mayoral candidate Boris Johnson advocates replacing bendy buses with '21st century Routemaster'** December *Autocar* **magazine publishes designs for a new bus**	May **Johnson wins mayoral election** July **Public bus-design competition launched at London Transport Museum (LTM)** December **Capoco and Foster + Partners/Aston Martin announced as winners of professional strand of competition**

MCW Metrobus 1979

Sharing with the Titan the distinction of being London's standard bus throughout the 1980s, the Metrobus was an off-the-shelf design built by Metro Cammell Weymann. It was ordered in large numbers by London Transport, and some examples remained in service until 2004. By the time of its appearance on the capital's streets, however, the status of bus travel had declined even further, with diminishing revenues ruling out investment in new bus designs geared to the requirements of Londoners, and political pressures eventually leading to the gradual privatisation of the London bus network from 1984 onwards. Nevertheless, in contrast to the rival Titan, the Metrobus enjoyed a ready market elsewhere in the UK and abroad.

Dennis Trident 1999
Enviro400H 2008

Growing concerns over air quality in central London, together with the arrival of a London mayor with a clear environmental policy, led to the emergence of cleaner and quieter buses in the post-2000 period. The hybrid Enviro400H, by Alexander Dennis, evolved from the company's Trident and Enviro400 double-deckers, which had been serving London since the turn of the millennium and the mid-2000s respectively. Series-hybrid operation not only reduces emissions but also recuperates energy during each of the bus's frequent stops, helping to lower fuel consumption by some 30 per cent compared with a conventional diesel design. Yet despite the easy low-floor entry of these buses, the result of a desire to make the bus fleet more accessible, the travelling public has not warmed to their brash, clinical interiors.

Far left
The MCW Metrobus was typical of the open-market designs that the fragmented London Transport was forced to buy during the privatisation era of the 1980s.

Above
The low-floor Dennis Trident series has been widely deployed in London. The later Enviro and hybrid versions offer fuel and emissions savings.

February **Announcement of tender for design and development contract published in** *Official Journal of the EU*

February **Prizewinning designs from public competition displayed at LTM**

March **Pre-qualification questionnaires issued to aspiring bidders**

May **Six bus manufacturers invited to negotiate with TfL**

June **Official tender specification issued**

June **Bidders' conference**

August **Deadline for bid submissions extended**

October **Final negotiations with shortlisted bidders**

December **Wrightbus announced as contract winner; Boris Johnson promises bus will arrive in 2011**

January **Contract signed with Wrightbus**

January **Heatherwick Studio formally engaged as design consultant**

May **Exterior concepts approved; Johnson unveils final design**

November **Wrightbus completes mock-up of bus**

November **Mock-up moved to LTM's depot in Acton, west London; Johnson photographed on rear platform**

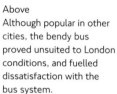

Above
Although popular in other cities, the bendy bus proved unsuited to London conditions, and fuelled dissatisfaction with the bus system.

Above, far right
The Eclipse Gemini has been one of London's staple buses for the early twenty-first century; hybrid versions were among the world's first.

Mercedes-Benz Citaro 2002

With the arrival of Mercedes' 18-metre-long (60 feet) articulated single-decker, otherwise known as the bendy bus, London buses suddenly became a hot political topic – and they have remained a talking point ever since. Introduced in the wake of the much-loved Routemasters, which were worn out, expensive to operate and incompatible with accessibility legislation, the bendy bus carried 140 passengers – most of them standing – and permitted entry through any of its three doors, thus providing truly rapid boarding. The operators loved the Citaro's efficiency, but it was politically unpopular, fare evasion was claimed to be rife, and the bus was widely vilified in the press. It was eventually hounded out of service following incoming mayor Boris Johnson's 2008 election commitment to replace it with a latter-day Routemaster.

Wrightbus Eclipse Gemini 2009

Very much the state of the art in off-the-shelf double-decker bus design, the Eclipse family of buses has been serving London for many years and in many different guises, in terms of both engineering and exterior detailing. All models are distinguished by an enormous panoramic windscreen, elliptical in shape and occupying almost the entire front face of the bus. Hybrid versions employ the Volvo ISAM parallel hybrid system, which contrasts with the series configuration used on buses made by Wrightbus. As in the case of all driver-only double-deckers, entry is through the front doors, and a single staircase serves the upper deck.

May **First working prototype of new bus tested at Millbrook Proving Ground, Bedfordshire**

November **Johnson visits Wrightbus factory in Ballymena, NI, and drives first prototype**

December **Last bendy bus service in London**

December **Public launch of new bus outside City Hall, London; bus driven to Trafalgar Square**

February **New bus begins public service on route 38**

May **Boris Johnson re-elected as mayor, commits to ordering production buses**

May **Johnson opens bus-production facility at Wrightbus**

September **TfL board places order for 600 buses**

January **Johnson announces that route 24 will be first to run new bus exclusively**

April **First production buses leave manufacturing plant**

June–September **Route 24 adopts the new bus; route 11 begins to convert to the new bus**

December **Route 390 gets the new bus**

Last of 600 new buses set to be delivered

Wrightbus Pulsar 2 2010

Although only a single-decker, the Pulsar 2 is a significant vehicle in the story of London's buses, being fuelled by hydrogen and consequently producing zero emissions. Built by Wrightbus in Belfast and powered by a fuel cell, which provides current for its electric motor, the Pulsar 2 operates on the RV1 tourist route (Tower Gateway station to Covent Garden). The bus is smooth and near silent, and can run for 18 hours before needing to refuel at TfL's new hydrogen hub in east London. The organisation says that hydrogen buses are proving themselves from an operational perspective, with operating ranges and performance comparable to those of diesel buses. The challenge is the higher capital cost, which currently needs additional financial support to make the buses viable.

Wrightbus New Routemaster 2012

Rarely, if ever, has so much emotion and political charge been wrapped up in a single vehicle, let alone a London bus. But such was the hysteria surrounding the bendy buses that the idea of a return to the glory days of the Routemaster not only proved a vote winner in the 2008 mayoral election, but also resulted in an appealing mode of transport for modern Londoners. Stylish, smooth and impeccably kitted out, the designer-sculpted New Routemaster promises to recapture the hearts of the travelling public, as well as reducing harmful emissions by 40 per cent, in comparison to a standard bus, thanks to its innovative series-hybrid propulsion system.

Far left
Following an in-service trial with hydrogen buses in 2004, TfL began operating eight zero-emission Wrightbus Pulsars on a permanent basis on the RV1 route.

Above
The New Routemaster is the first bus since its 1959 mentor to have been expressly designed around Londoners' requirements. Its stylish design has been seen as a return to quality values in public transport.

A Century of Buses

Statistics covering more than a century of London's bus operations show how the shape and role of bus travel in the capital have evolved. Passenger numbers trebled between the two world wars, aided by a rapidly expanding fleet of buses. The sharp dip around 1940 reflects the reduction in travel brought about by the Second World War and its attendant fuel shortages, while the steady climb after the war reveals a strong demand for public transport, itself a reflection of a rejuvenated economy focusing on exports and depriving UK buyers of the new cars they desired.

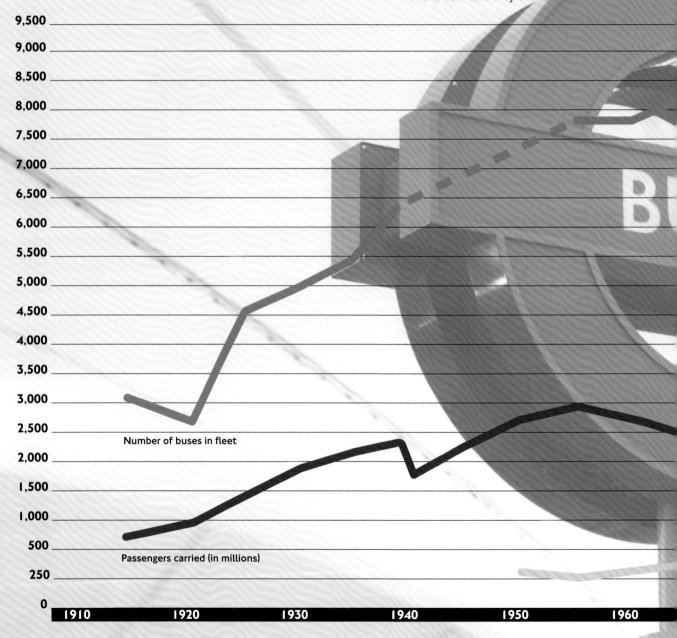

Number of buses in fleet

Passengers carried (in millions)

9,500
9,000
8,500
8,000
7,500
7,000
6,500
6,000
5,500
5,000
4,500
4,000
3,500
3,000
2,500
2,000
1,500
1,000
500
250
0

1910   1920   1930   1940   1950   1960

Although the damaging bus strike of 1958 had a material effect on bus-passenger numbers, one thing is clear: rising numbers of private cars on London's roads in the 1950s and 1960s were sapping demand for bus travel, as well as adding to congestion, which in turn made bus travel slower. Much more consistent over the decades is the number of vehicle miles travelled, despite the rising number of buses in service, especially after the turn of the millennium. This would point towards buses being used for shorter journeys rather than longer trips.

It should be noted that changes in accounting methods, alterations to London's administrative boundaries and varying definitions of vehicle fleets mean that it is hard to make direct comparisons between figures from different decades. This graphical representation is of necessity an approximation derived from the official figures available.

Source: Annual Reports of London Transport, Transport for London and its predecessor bodies

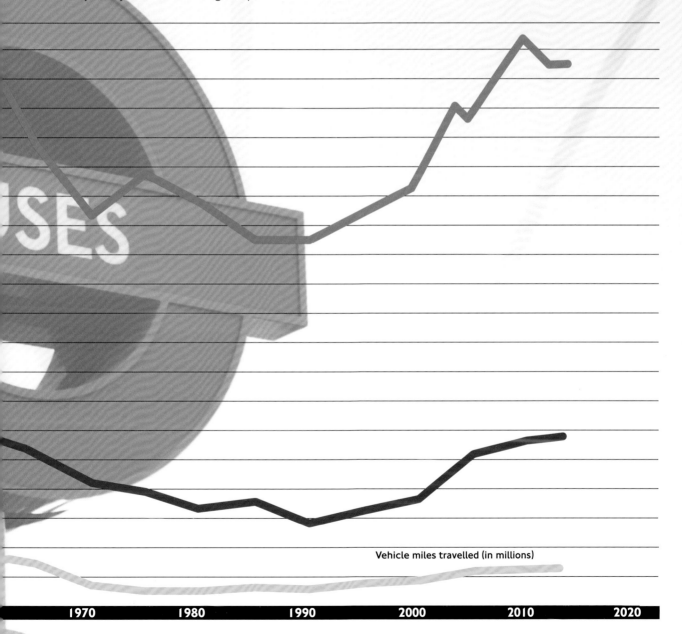

Vehicle miles travelled (in millions)

1970   1980   1990   2000   2010   2020

Facts and Figures

With 6.5 million journeys made on them every weekday, London's buses carry the equivalent of a quarter of the world's population every year. These and other London-bus statistics make for astonishing reading.

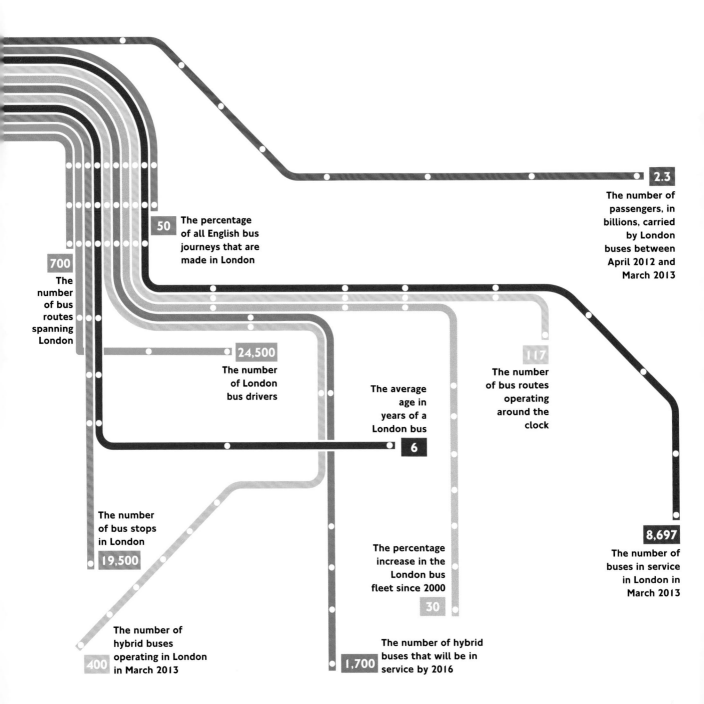

2.3
The number of passengers, in billions, carried by London buses between April 2012 and March 2013

50
The percentage of all English bus journeys that are made in London

700
The number of bus routes spanning London

24,500
The number of London bus drivers

117
The number of bus routes operating around the clock

The average age in years of a London bus
6

The number of bus stops in London
19,500

The percentage increase in the London bus fleet since 2000
30

8,697
The number of buses in service in London in March 2013

The number of hybrid buses operating in London in March 2013
400

1,700 The number of hybrid buses that will be in service by 2016

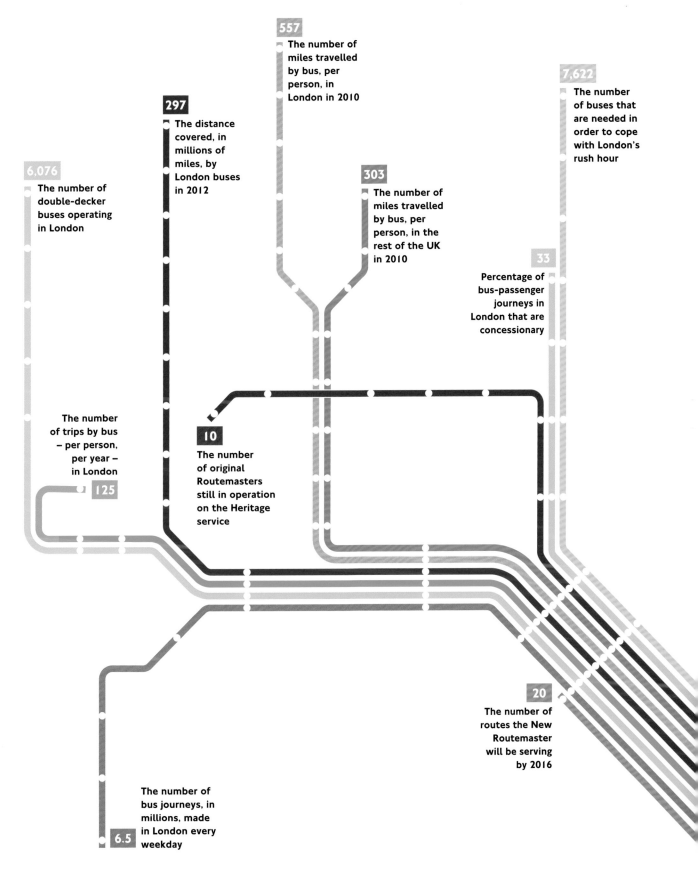

557
The number of miles travelled by bus, per person, in London in 2010

297
The distance covered, in millions of miles, by London buses in 2012

7,622
The number of buses that are needed in order to cope with London's rush hour

303
The number of miles travelled by bus, per person, in the rest of the UK in 2010

6,076
The number of double-decker buses operating in London

33
Percentage of bus-passenger journeys in London that are concessionary

The number of trips by bus – per person, per year – in London
125

10
The number of original Routemasters still in operation on the Heritage service

20
The number of routes the New Routemaster will be serving by 2016

The number of bus journeys, in millions, made in London every weekday
6.5

A NEW
LON

2

BUS FOR DON

The Public Competition

Pages 40–41
The public competition to design a new bus for London was launched with this simple but elegant logo, which was used extensively in both presentations and documentation.

A few minutes before midnight on Friday, 2 May 2008, Boris Johnson was formally declared the winner of the London mayoral election. The idea of reviving the Routemaster was no longer a vague aspiration: it had become a concrete commitment, pushed to the top of the new mayor's to-do list by his insistence during his campaign on immediate action.

And, true to his promise, Johnson did indeed launch a competition; however, it was not quite the competition that readers of his manifesto had been led to expect. Instead of inviting the 'world's leading designers and engineers' to draw up their proposals for a brand-new bus, as described in his manifesto, the Mayor put out two very different calls — each of which went out to vastly broader groups of people.

London Mayor Boris Johnson launches the New Bus for London public competition in July 2008. The venue is the London Transport Museum in Covent Garden.

Commissioner of Transport for London Sir Peter Hendy, Mayor Boris Johnson and David Brown, former managing director of surface transport, pose in front of a classic Routemaster.

David Hampson-Ghani, who up to that point had been working on upgrading TfL's Dial-a-Ride service, was called in at short notice to project-manage the competition process. Charged with taking swift action to satisfy the Mayor's requirement to get the project moving, Hampson-Ghani and the TfL team decided that the competition would be open to the public, with one contest for professionals and another for amateurs. The so-called Imagine category was open to everyone, from schoolchildren and students to budding inventors, and called for their ideas and images of future bus travel. While this category carried a series of modest prizes, a much more substantial headline prize of £25,000 was on offer to the winner of the Design category, in which colleges, universities, studios and practising designers were invited to put forward professional proposals, complete with technical drawings and complying with a detailed technical specification.

'The response was incredible', recalls Hampson-Ghani. 'We hadn't done much publicity – just a couple of stories in the *Evening Standard* and *Metro* – but we got more than 700 entries, and from all over the world. Even India, China, Singapore, the US, Hong Kong. Some of the work was of a very high standard, even in the Imagine category.'

All the while, however, TfL executives were secure in the knowledge that the terms of the competition did not commit them to adopting any of the ideas submitted – even the winning ones. Clearly stated on the entry form was the proviso that the copyright to the entries would reside with TfL, thus ruling out any potential issues to do with intellectual property rights.

The judging panel, consisting of senior executives from TfL and the mayor's office, announced the results of the competition in December 2008. A remarkable spectrum of ideas was revealed, ranging from

A NEW BUS FOR
LONDON

Competition rules -
A new bus for London

Design category

1. Entries in the Design category may be for the whole-bus ('whole-bus design') or for one or more features or parts of the bus ('element design').

2. Whole-bus design entries must comply with all of the following requirements:

   (a) The design must be for a red double-decker bus with at least one internal staircase.

   (b) The design must incorporate an open access platform entrance/exit located at the rear near-side corner and at least one other entrance/exit with double doors (similar to the side doors in the middle of a modern London double-decker bus)

   (c) The bus must be operated with a second crew member

   (d) The total passenger capacity must be at least 72, with a mix of seated and standing passengers

   (e) The design must incorporate all compulsory elements in Table 1 of the Vehicle Specification Guidelines tfl.gov.uk/anewbusspecifications

   (f) The design must incorporate a low floor

   (g) The design must be practical and economic and capable of being put into mass production

3. Element design entries must focus on one or more of the design features required for whole-bus entries (listed in rule 2 above)

4. All entries in the Design category must include the following documents as a minimum:

   (a) A checklist showing how the entry is compliant with the requirements in rule 2 (for whole-bus designs) or 3 (for element designs)

   (b) A package of detailed design documents. For whole bus designs this must include plans, elevations, seating layouts, exterior and interior visualisations (including front and side views). These detailed drawings must also be provided for element designs to the extent they are relevant to the feature or part of the bus being designed

MAYOR OF LONDON   Transport for London

A NEW BUS FOR
LONDON

Competition rules -
A new bus for Lond...

Design categor...

4. (c) A detailed description of the reasoning and justification behind the design or design explaining in particular why the given approach has been adopted and any features included in the design in addition to the minimum requirements

5. All entries must be submitted with a completed official entry form which can be found at tfl.gov.uk/anewbusentryform

6. Entrants must state on the entry form that they are submitting their entry in the Design category. Entries cannot be submitted in both the Design category and the Imagine category. If an entry in the Design category does not comply with the rules for the Design category but complies with the rules for the Imagine category, it may be considered for a prize in the Imagine category.

7. Entries must be in English

MAYOR OF LONDON   Transport for London

Entry forms for the New Bus for London competition were clear in specifying the key features required for a Routemaster successor: red bodywork, an open rear platform and at least one staircase.

the outlandish to the brilliantly simple and clever. Hampson-Ghani remembers being particularly impressed by the comments and ideas from children and schools: 'There were things like play areas, tables, computer games and such like, but one that struck me as particularly brilliant was the suggestion that there should be handrails lower down. Children are always being told they must give up their seat if an adult wants to sit down, but there's never anything for the child to hold on to.'

Most encouraging of all, in Hampson-Ghani's view, was the sheer excitement and enthusiasm that was evident both in the children's drawings and in the reactions of the winning school classes when they came to the launch of the real bus on 16 December 2011, some three years later. 'At the end of the day it was just a bus,' observes Hampson-Ghani, 'but it had really inspired the children's imagination. Some of them were interviewed by the BBC and they were so excited about the design, even though it was nothing to do with their own drawings. We need to remember that these are the passengers of the future.'

The professional side of the competition was altogether more in-depth, requiring not just technical presentations for the complete bus but data and justifications, too. Again, for TfL the intent was to identify real ideas that could be used on real projects, or be put on the back burner for future developments. Hampson-Ghani was again impressed by the work, especially that of 'a one-man band, a guy in his bedroom', who presented a meticulously worked-up and thoroughly professional proposal, complete with renderings, specifications and engineering arguments. At the end of the judges' deliberations two proposals were declared joint

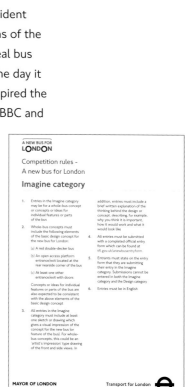

A NEW BUS FOR
LONDON

Competition rules -
A new bus for London

Imagine category

1. Entries in the Imagine category may be for a whole-bus concept or concepts or ideas for individual features or parts of the bus

2. Whole-bus concepts must include the following elements of the basic design concept for the new bus for London:

   (a) A red double-decker bus

   (b) An open access platform entrance/exit located at the rear nearside corner of the bus

   (c) At least one other entrance/exit with doors

   Concepts or ideas for individual features or parts of the bus are also expected to be consistent with the above elements of the basic design concept

3. All entries in the Imagine category must include at least one sketch or drawing which gives a visual impression of the concept for the new bus (or feature of the bus). For whole-bus concepts, this could be an 'artist's impression' type drawing of the front and side views. In

   addition, entries must include a brief written explanation of the thinking behind the design or concept, describing, for example, why you think it is important, how it would work and what it would look like

4. All entries must be submitted with a completed official entry form which can be found at tfl.gov.uk/anewbusentryform

5. Entrants must state on the entry form that they are submitting their entry in the Imagine category. Submissions cannot be entered in both the Imagine category and the Design category

6. Entries must be in English

MAYOR OF LONDON   Transport for London

winners: one from established bus and truck design company Capoco, and the other from a high-profile partnership between international architects Foster + Partners and luxury sports car manufacturer Aston Martin.

What was striking about both winning designs was their similarity, Capoco's appearing to be a lightly reworked version of the design it had produced for *Autocar* magazine the year before. The Foster + Partners/Aston Martin proposal was much more rounded in appearance,

looking almost like a tram, and included such distinctly premium features as wooden floors and leather upholstery. Both designs aped the asymmetric half-cab frontal configuration of the original Routemaster, while Capoco's, so as to leave observers in no doubt whatsoever about the reference, even featured a pastiche of the original's grille and headlights.

In each case the treatment of the open rear platform was almost identical to that of the Routemaster. Both winning designs also featured a wide single side-entry door just aft of the front wheels, as well as the classic sideways-facing seating above the rear wheels on the lower deck. Yet, according to Hampson-Ghani, where several of the entries, including the winning Foster + Partners/Aston Martin proposal, would have been wrong for public service was in specifying a glass roof in order to lend an observation-deck atmosphere to the upper saloon. 'We were convinced these were unfeasible,' he explains, 'not just from the point of view of solar heat gain but also

because of the extra weight and the effect on structural integrity.'

Another notable aspect of the twin competitions was that, with the exception of Capoco, no front-running bus companies or noted industry professionals had submitted an entry. For some companies, concerned about protecting their designs, the contest must have been too public; for others, it may have appeared too restrictive in its conditions, especially those relating to intellectual property rights. In any case, word had been circulating among Europe's leading bus builders that a different and much more prestigious research and design contract might be in the offing. From a purely commercial standpoint, it would make sense for any company with serious aspirations of playing in this premier league to keep its intentions secret and wait for the announcement of the real contest.

So although some may have been disappointed at the public contests' failure to attract many big names, the initiative was nevertheless highly successful in drawing attention to bus travel, fulfilling Boris Johnson's election promises and, crucially, buying time for the procurement team to lay foundations for the actual commissioning process. Not only did it raise general awareness of buses and bus design, but also it enabled the public to buy in to the whole idea of a new bus, rebuilding the long-lost sense of involvement. And, perhaps more importantly still, it promised at last to lay to rest the contention often attributed, perhaps apocryphally, to former prime minister Margaret Thatcher, and subsequently mocked by Johnson, that buses were only for losers.

Both the mainstream press and the business-to-business publications, such as *Coach and Bus Week*, followed the public competition with great interest, enthusiastically reporting on the prospects for a new Routemaster.

Opposite, top
The roll-call of twenty-seven different winners reflected the widespread interest in both parts of the competition: the Design category for professionals, and the Imagine category for the general public.

Opposite, bottom
Mike Weston, director of bus operations at TfL, poses for the camera with children from St Antony's Primary School in Forest Gate, north-east London. The school won a special award in honour of the fact that every pupil submitted an entry.

Design Category Prizewinners

	Whole Bus Design		Element Design
= 1st £25,000 each	**= 2nd** £10,000 each	**Merit** £2,000 each	**Merit** £1,000 each
Capoco Design Ltd	Héctor Serrano Studio	David Bradshaw	Lotti Duke
Foster + Partners/Aston Martin	Jamie Martin	Style to Design Ltd	Rhys Whyman
		Concrete All-Round Creative	
		LA:UK Design Ltd	
		Eric Woodcock	

Imagine Category Prizewinners

Age group	1st	2nd	3rd	Merit
<11	£200 bike voucher Experience session on bus driving simulator for 4	4 tickets to London Transport Museum + £50 voucher	4 tickets to London Transport Museum + £25 voucher	£25 voucher
	Thomas Staricoff Olivia Carrier	Luke Brennan	Yasmin Ali	Hanna Broadhurst Takeo Broadhurst
11–15	£300 bike voucher Experience session on bus driving simulator for 4	4 tickets to London Transport Museum + £50 voucher	4 tickets to London Transport Museum + £25 voucher	–
	Dolapo Okunlola	Ben Holmes	Albert Braid	
16–18	£500 bike voucher Experience session on bus driving simulator for 4	4 tickets to London Transport Museum + £50 voucher	4 tickets to London Transport Museum + £25 voucher	–
	Nicholas Cho	Craig Tomkins	Charlotte Taylor	
>18	£1,000	£500	£250	£100
	Frances Faulder	Matt Belcher	Alan Thorley	Laszlo Vas

Design Category

WHOLE BUS DESIGN
Joint first prize

Capoco Design Ltd, Wiltshire

Praised by the judges for its technical excellence, the Capoco submission was felt to be innovative and practical for production – a reflection, perhaps, of the real-world experience of its creators. Visually, the design had changed little since its first appearance in *Autocar* magazine a year earlier.

WHOLE BUS DESIGN

Joint first prize

Foster + Partners, London/ Aston Martin, Warwickshire

More modern and more immediately striking than the Capoco design, the Foster + Partners/ Aston Martin entry pleased the judges with its architectural approach and design references to the RT, predecessor of the original Routemaster, especially its wooden flooring.

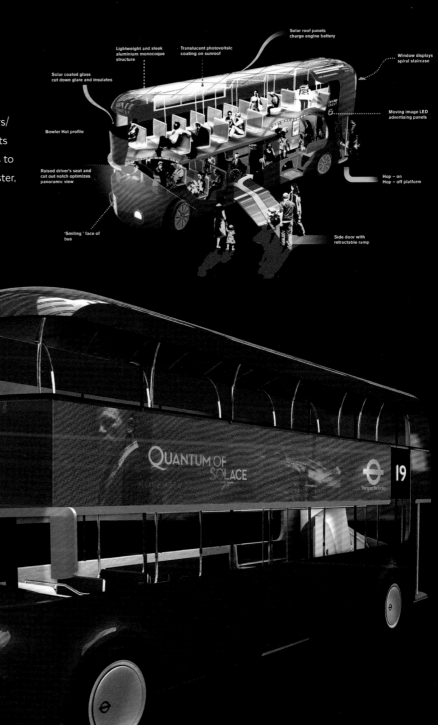

Solar roof panels charge engine battery

Lightweight and sleek aluminium monocoque structure

Translucent photovoltaic coating on sunroof

Window displays spiral staircase

Solar coated glass cut down glare and insulates

Moving image LED advertising panels

Bowler Hat profile

Raised driver's seat and cut out notch optimizes panoramic view

Hop – on Hop – off platform

'Smiling ' face of bus

Side door with retractable ramp

WHOLE BUS DESIGN
Joint second prize

Héctor Serrano Studio, London

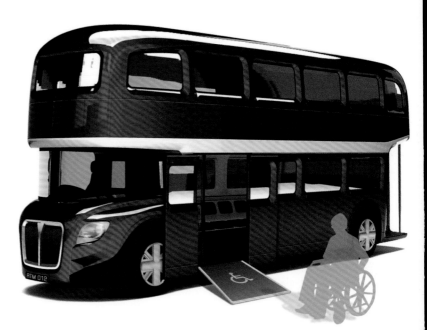

The joint runner-up entry from the Héctor Serrano Studio was praised by the judging panel for its modernised take on the classic Routemaster look, and for its wide doors, stairs and aisles. Cantilever seat mountings would have eased the task of floor cleaning.

WHOLE BUS DESIGN
Joint second prize

Jamie Martin, London

This proved an early favourite with the judges, who noted its bold and original reinterpretation of the original Routemaster lines, as well as such details as the design of the handrail and the novel safety barrier for the rear platform.

WHOLE BUS DESIGN
Merit

David Bradshaw, Nottinghamshire

The engineering-led solution proposed by David Bradshaw earned him a merit for its hub motors and for a seating layout able to accommodate 100 passengers.

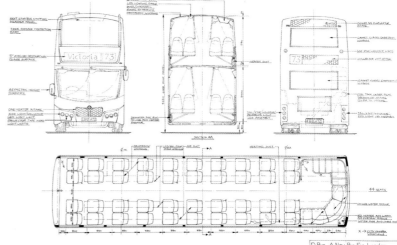

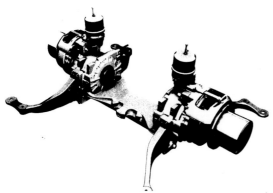

WHOLE BUS DESIGN
Merit

Style to Design Ltd, Nottinghamshire

First impressions of the entry from Style to Design are of a classic Routemaster updated in detail only. However, the judges praised such features as the hybrid drive system (using super-capacitors) and the easily negotiated staircase.

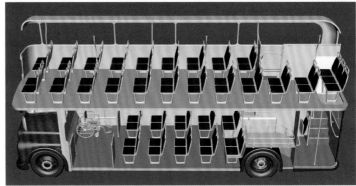

WHOLE BUS DESIGN
Merit

Concrete All-Round Creative, Belgium

This striking solution from Belgium caught the judges' attention, with its smooth, product-design looks breaking the mould of traditional bus design – including that of the classic Routemaster.

WHOLE BUS DESIGN
Merit

LA:UK Design Ltd, Cheshire

LA:UK's design was praised for its meticulous execution and modern interpretation of features from the original Routemaster. The novel curved theme of the entrances was particularly appreciated, as was the rear-platform door arrangement.

WHOLE BUS DESIGN
Merit

Eric Woodcock, Merseyside

Bus engineer Eric Woodcock took a novel approach
with his design, placing the driver in a central
position and employing front-wheel drive. Twin rear
axles and a balcony platform at the rear are further
stand-out features.

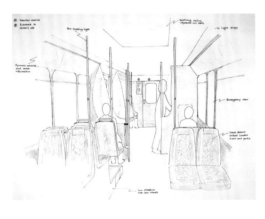

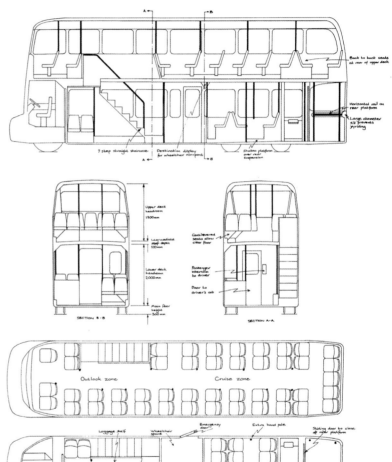

ELEMENT DESIGN
Merit

Lotti Duke, Lancashire

The first of two merits awarded for the design of individual elements went to Lotti Duke for her elegant Oyster-card reader and passenger information systems.

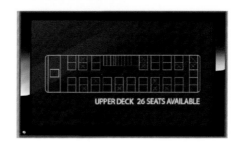

UPPER DECK 26 SEATS AVAILABLE

TICKETS

Oyster Top up

Day Rider £4.50

Single Journey £2

ELEMENT DESIGN
Merit

Rhys Whyman, Hertfordshire

Rhys Whyman earned a merit for his imaginative door designs, and for the inspired detailing of the seating, hand poles and other interior elements.

WHOLE BUS DESIGN
Entrant

Jan Kaplicky

This colourful vision for a future London bus was submitted by the late Jan Kaplicky (1937–2009) of Future Systems fame, the radical architectural practice behind the Lord's Cricket Ground media centre and the Selfridges building in Birmingham.

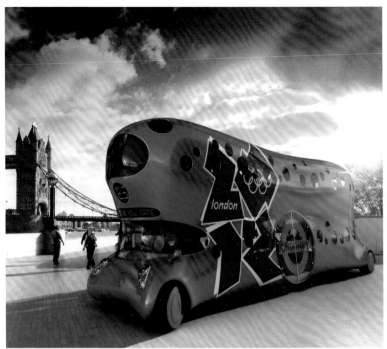

WHOLE BUS DESIGN
Entrant

Matthew Heywood

Matthew Heywood, also connected with Future Systems, developed a similarly organic form for a new bus, albeit one with a much narrower upper deck and a Routemaster-style half-cab for the driver.

WHOLE BUS DESIGN
Entrant

BAND
(Bureau of Architecture, Networks and Design)

This architectural practice adopted a deliberately provocative approach, combining the exterior design of a classic Routemaster with a fully glazed upper deck incorporating twelve bath tubs for commuters with an acute sense of cleanliness — and humour.

WHOLE BUS DESIGN
Entrant

Pope Wainwright

This London-based design and branding studio, which specialises in retail environments, squared off the classic Routemaster's lines and dramatically extended the glazing to incorporate the entire roof, including the canopy above the rear stairs.

Imagine Category

IMAGINE
Under 11s

Joint winners of the under-eleven category were Thomas Staricoff from Brighton, already a bus enthusiast at the age of nine, and Olivia Carrier, whose bus has flower-shaped wheels. Other novel ideas submitted in this age group included buses shaped like a teapot, a rabbit and the Albert Hall.

Thomas Staricoff
Joint first place

Olivia Carrier
Joint first place

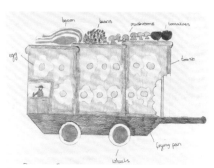

Jasel Patel
Entrant

Maya Acha
Entrant

Rahul Kanani
Entrant

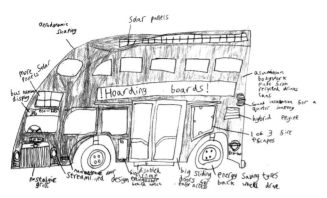

Luke Brennan
Second place

Hanna Broadhurst
Merit

Yasmin Ali
Third place

Takeo Broadhurst
Merit

Serena Mirpuri
Entrant

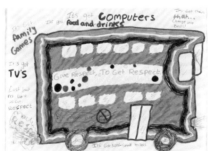

Jennifer Ese
Entrant

Zane Edwin
Entrant

IMAGINE

11–15

The eleven-to-fifteen age group brought a more disciplined approach to bus design, showing a clear reverence for the original Routemaster, and incorporating such key details as the rear open platform.

Dolapo Okunlola
First place

Ben Holmes
Second place

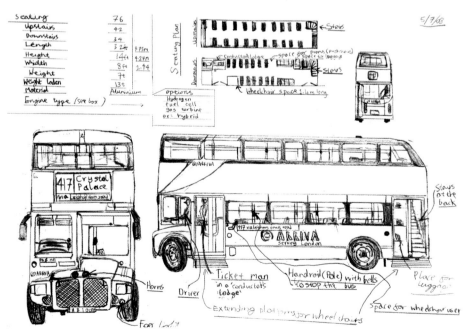

Albert Braid
Third place

IMAGINE
16–18

In the sixteen-to-eighteen age group, the winning entry, from self-confessed automobile design fanatic Nicholas Cho, features an imaginative expandable interior intended to minimise the bus's footprint in traffic. Craig Tomkins, an aspiring transport designer, took second place with his elegantly streamlined design, while Charlotte Taylor earned third prize for her more conventional study.

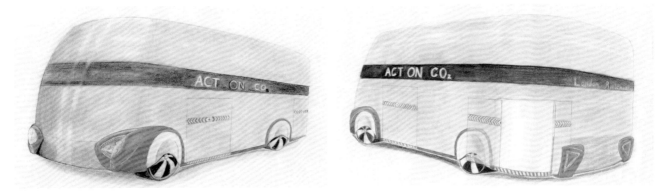

Nicholas Cho
First place

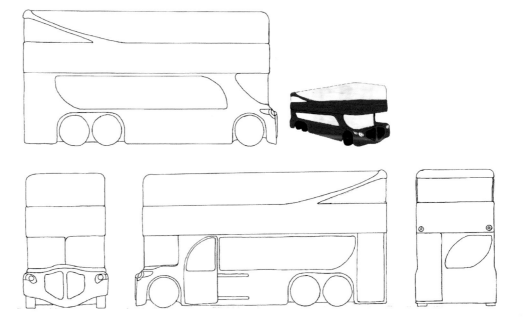

Craig Tomkins
Second place

Charlotte Taylor
Third place

IMAGINE
Over 18s

Graphic designer Frances Faulder took the top prize in the over-eighteens division for her smooth double-decker described as a 'practical but beautiful object' — one that would give passengers an unimpeded view of the city. Second-place Matt Belcher's design aims to combine innovation with respect for the city's transport heritage, while Alan Thorley and Laszlo Vas bring a car designer's eye and the shock of a dramatic, layered 3D approach respectively.

Frances Faulder
First place

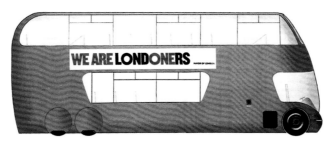

Matt Belcher
Second place

Alan Thorley
Third place

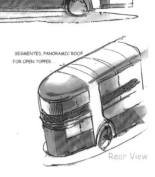

Laszlo Vas
Merit

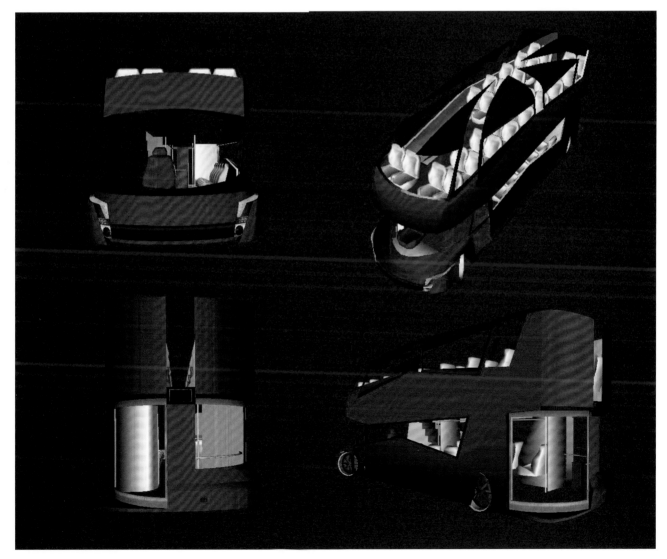

The Tendering Process

It is late 2008 and the winners of the public competitions – and, indeed, the Mayor and his team – are relishing the media spotlight: everyone is talking about buses, which are now enjoying a much higher and more positive profile than ever before. In dramatic contrast to the traditionally grey and institutional image of public transport, and of buses in particular, glamorous and prestigious household names are now involved: Aston Martin, Foster + Partners, and *Autocar* magazine and its appetite for high-horsepower Bugattis and Ferraris. And however insistent the questioning by some of the Mayor's political opponents, there is an undoubted sense of anticipation and excitement, a recognition of real possibilities ahead.

Yet all the while, well shielded from the media's gaze, senior TfL officials had been busy behind the scenes on a much more serious and business-focused task: preparing the ground for the real bus. Teams of experts had been informally sounding out the leading European bus manufacturers to provide TfL with the background that would help it draw up the specifications for the really big contest that it knew was coming up. For the competition that would really count was the public procurement exercise to determine which organisations would design, develop and produce the first prototype batch of neo-Routemasters – and have the capacity to manufacture up to 600 of them if the in-service trials proved successful.

As a public procurement exercise with a likely final bill approaching eight figures, the process was

Pages 64–65
Traffic circulates around the IMAX cinema in Waterloo, south London. Clearly visible in this bird's-eye view are a bendy bus and three different types of double-decker.

Variety in style: the proliferation in London bus types is well illustrated in this street view, with two different single-deckers sandwiched between a pair of double-deckers, also of different types.

governed by a strict set of rules, both internal and external: the invitation to tender had to be announced in the *Official Journal of the European Union* for a specified period of time, the technical specifications had to be closely defined, and the exact criteria for assessing the rival bids had to be laid down.

As part of the first-round tendering process, potential bidders were given a packaged-up version of the entries from the public competitions, with the recommendation to take note of all of them and, if so desired, to make free use of the ideas they contained. What TfL steered clear of, however, was making any specific suggestions or pointing to any particular entries. 'We didn't want to direct', says David Hampson-Ghani, by now project manager for the whole New Routemaster programme. 'It was a balance we had to strike between being proscriptive and allowing creativity.'

Also as part of the first-round process, TfL 'strongly advised' interested bidders to team up with an industrial-design or product-design organisation right from the beginning, not as an afterthought. This was the initiative of Daniel Moylan, who had recently been appointed as a TfL board member by the Mayor, and who soon became its deputy chairman. 'We wanted them to take on some new thinking,' explains Hampson-Ghani, 'otherwise we were going to get the buses we've always had, but with a little bit of tinkering at the end. We made it as clear as we could that that was what we wanted to happen, without forcing it to happen.'

The timetable of the Europe-wide procurement process saw the official announcement of the tender in February 2009; it ran for a month and a half. Pre-qualification submissions helped screen out candidates who were not up to the job, and six interested parties went forward and were invited to take part in the next round, described as a negotiated procurement exercise. These six companies were Alexander Dennis, EvoBus/Mercedes-Benz, Hispano Carrocera (since taken over by Tata, which controls Jaguar Land Rover), Optare, Scania and Wrightbus. Volvo was one of the companies that declined to take part.

TfL then took the unusual step of inviting all the contenders to a bidders' conference, something that unsettled some of the hard-line negotiators on the teams. 'We got them all in a room, the same room, and went over the whole project again in an open forum', explains Hampson-Ghani. 'That was very unusual and initially they didn't like it, but it ended up as an extremely useful exercise. There were also private rooms available if they didn't want to expose their own ignorance or lack of understanding, or reveal their ideas.'

Tender Specification

The formal tender was launched in May 2009 and called for, among other technical features, a target passenger capacity of eighty-seven, twin staircases and an open rear platform that could be closed off when the bus was being run in the non-conductor mode. Crucially, the technical specifications were defined largely in terms of performance and results, leaving the companies free to choose the powertrain technologies they felt were best suited to the task.

Mike Weston, director of bus operations at TfL, was a leading voice in shaping the requirements that were eventually written in to the tender.

Engineering First, then Style

New Routemaster project manager David Hampson-Ghani on why TfL's bid teams wanted to test the technology before they saw the shape

'We told the bidders we wanted an iconic bus, but that we wanted to evaluate the bids first on technical, commercial and contractual compliance. Only after this would we ask them to present their aesthetic design. We made it clear that we didn't want to see any imagery of any sort before they were selected to offer that. Number one, we didn't want them to waste time on it, and, secondly, we didn't want to be influenced by a pretty picture.

'Our philosophy was this: let's get the engineering right, let's get the technology right – and surely we can wrap a design on to that. We knew if we saw something, you couldn't put it back in the bottle. On the technical side we needed to ask, "Is the structure going to work? Is that maintainable? Is that durable?" We didn't want to have to do that with someone saying, "Ah, but I like that one best."

'We got to the point where we said we would disqualify anyone who showed us a picture. It's easier to judge the pictures than the engineering, but first and foremost we had to have a bus that worked. Looking pretty was in all honesty the second consideration.'

London is different from other cities, he explains, not only because it is geographically large but also because it has 'a lot of ons and offs' – a lot of people who change modes of transport or change buses within the city. Most other large cities are more radial in their structure, with people making a single journey in and another back out, rather than travelling within the central zone. Translated into bus terms, this means large numbers of people must be able to board or leave the bus as quickly as possible. 'For some while', says Weston, 'our policy has been to have buses with twin doors; in other cities they're usually single-door. On high-frequency routes like the 38 [Clapton Pond to Victoria Bus Station], buses come every 1½ or 2 minutes – there are huge numbers of people and we need to get them on and off fast.'

The project's specifications were directed at these high-intensity central routes. 'Our fundamental requirement at TfL', explains Sir Peter Hendy, 'was to have three doors for maximum boarding speed: this had been the best feature of the articulated [bendy] bus, and we wanted it for the New Routemaster. The Mayor wanted an open rear platform, so as a consequence we ended up with a clever arrangement that included both.' The whole primary contract was framed as a research and development project leading to a batch of prototypes, but without any commitment to buying further examples.

EvoBus/Mercedes-Benz and Scania pulled out after the bidders' conference, which was held in June, leaving the remaining four companies' bids to undergo rigorous examination. Hispano Carrocera and Optare were next to leave the process, and there then followed a long series of negotiations and clarifications with Alexander Dennis and

Wrightbus, leading up to a deadline for final submissions in December.

The intention at TfL had always been to assess the bids on their technical and performance merits alone, and to leave aesthetic qualities out of the equation. Only then would the companies be asked to present their designs for the bus. As Hampson-Ghani recalls, 'We wanted an iconic bus, but we didn't want to make the [initial] selection on the basis of imagery or be influenced by a pretty picture. Our philosophy was, "Let's get the technology right, let's get the engineering right, and then we're sure to be able to wrap a design on to that".'

The framework for the scoring system was clearly laid out, with a host of different factors given different weightings. Of the final score for each bid, 50 per cent of the marks would be for technical compliance, 40 per cent for commercial compliance and the remaining 10 per cent for contractual compliance. And because of the high public profile of the contract, the procurement evaluation process had to be absolutely watertight and beyond challenge when the final decision came to be made.

And the Winner Is ...

Although the announcement of the winner was made by press release, when the metaphorical envelope was opened to reveal Wrightbus's name, there must have been considerable surprise: Alexander Dennis had been very confident in its bid, having brought on board — at the last minute and under the radar — the two winners of the professional strand of the public competition, Capoco and Foster + Partners/Aston Martin.

According to TfL executives, the Wrightbus bid was the more expensive, but it was technically better and had superior packaging (the way in which the engine and powertrain components are fitted within the chassis and body). Importantly, too, it was felt that Wrightbus was more open to suggestions than its rival. Hampson-Ghani quotes the example of drive-by noise limits: TfL had specified a limit of 75 decibels, which Wrightbus was brave enough to flag up as unachievable. To demonstrate

"I just asked him if he'd consider becoming a bus driver if he lost the election in 2012!"

Mayor Boris Johnson and the New Bus for London project enjoyed a high public profile throughout the project's formative years, as shown by this Gerard Whyman cartoon taken from *RouteOne* magazine (18 November 2010).

its point, engineers at Wrightbus rolled an engine-less bus past the microphones at the specified speed, and it exceeded the 75-decibel limit on tyre noise alone. Accepting its error, TfL raised the noise target to 76 decibels.

The next step was to view the designs, as opposed to the engineering proposals. The so-called beauty parade produced a sense of disappointment among TfL officials, who felt that both the Alexander Dennis and the Wrightbus in-house designs smacked too much of the old; of the two surprise extra concepts wheeled out by Alexander Dennis, the Capoco example was seen as heavy and unconvincing, while the Foster + Partners/Aston Martin alternative was judged too tricky to build.

TfL, however, had anticipated just such a situation, and had made plans accordingly. During the tendering process, bidders had agreed to allow a TfL-nominated design consultant to join the project, at TfL's expense, should the in-house designs not come up to scratch. As luck would have it, Daniel Moylan, in his previous capacity as deputy council leader of the Royal Borough of Kensington and Chelsea, had worked with an innovative London design firm on some highly successful newspaper kiosks in Sloane Square and Earls Court. This small but respected design house was one of those informally approached, and, although best known at that stage for its furniture and unusual architecture, the studio would later shoot to fame as the creator of the Olympic Cauldron in 2012.

So it was that the TfL board met on 18 December 2009 to appoint Wrightbus as the builder of the New Routemaster, with Heatherwick Studio as design consultants charged with ensuring the creation of an iconic, twenty-first-century successor to the original Routemaster. The mandatory award notification and standstill letter were issued to all the bidders, no challenges were received within the stipulated ten-day period, and the scene was now set for the project to proceed.

The Design

With the contract to design, develop and deliver six prototype buses signed and sealed between TfL and Wrightbus early in 2010, it was time to get the project moving. The sense of urgency was made all the more real by Mayor Boris Johnson's pre-election promise to have the heir to the Routemaster running on the streets of London by the end of his first term in office. Few needed to consult the calendar to realise that this meant a development period, from first sketch to final sign-off, of barely twenty-four months. This timeline would have posed a considerable challenge even in the case of a simple family hatchback, but for such a complex and fully accountable public procurement project as a London bus, it represented a daunting task indeed.

The stakes were raised still further by the project's high public profile and the novel arrangement between the contractors. Under the deal clinched between the two organisations at the turn of the year, Wrightbus would carry full responsibility for delivering the bus to the satisfaction of TfL, in both technical and visual terms. Heatherwick Studio, as design consultant, would propose design initiatives to TfL, which would then approve them and pass them on to Wrightbus; at no stage in the proceedings would Wrightbus directly accept instruction from Heatherwick. Implicit in this arrangement, however, was that Heatherwick was the design leader, and that Wrightbus's role was to make the studio's designs realisable.

What made the arrangement more unusual still was the fact that London-based Heatherwick Studio had no experience of automotive design or regulations, while Wrightbus – located some 800 kilometres (500 miles) from TfL

Below and opposite, left Thomas Heatherwick, pictured here on the front cover of the January/February 2012 edition of *The Economist*'s *Intelligent Life* magazine, founded his studio in 1994. Specialising in architecture, urban infrastructure, sculpture and design, the studio shot to fame with the award-winning UK Pavilion for the 2010 World Expo in Shanghai, and the Olympic Cauldron for the London 2012 Olympics.

Pages 72–73
The New Routemaster's glazed staircases and warm interior lighting give it the allure of a modern building or the interior of a smart department store. Designer Stuart Wood likens the bus to a slow-moving building.

across the water in Northern Ireland — was more used to working with outside design consultants under their direct control. Yet, says David Hampson-Ghani, this 'potentially explosive mix', with each of the three parties 'walking into the unknown', worked remarkably well in practice, with Heatherwick and Wrightbus working electronically side by side by the middle of the year. 'My role', Hampson-Ghani explains, 'was to oversee and to referee a lot of the decisions.'

While Wrightbus clearly had its work cut out delivering the technical side of the programme, especially in view of the massive variation of the original design likely to be proposed by Heatherwick Studio, the choice of Heatherwick as design consultant would at first appear even more counter-intuitive. Not so, argues Heatherwick's Stuart Wood, chief designer — alongside the studio's founder, Thomas Heatherwick — on the bus project: 'I think the attraction for TfL was our ability to apply creative and innovative thinking to any area. We don't have any automotive designers in the studio. Not one car designer; no one who has designed a bus. The appeal was that not having any baggage meant the hope of getting something fresh, not weighed down.'

The mayoral brief presented to Heatherwick Studio was the same as that given to Wrightbus, at least as far as the aesthetic side was concerned. As Hampson-Ghani explains, 'Heatherwick had to work with Wrightbus, within the constraints of the technical specification, to produce an overall look and feel for the inside and outside of the bus, and the componentry, that would help Wrightbus create an iconic twenty-first-century replacement for the Routemaster.'

That look and feel, at least in terms of the exterior of the bus, was surprisingly quick in arriving: by April 2010 everyone had agreed on the exterior theme, and this was presented to the Mayor, who, in Hampson-Ghani's words, 'bought the overall concept'. 'From then on,' he adds, somewhat understating the challenges that lay ahead, 'it was a matter of detailed design.'

Heatherwick Studio and Wrightbus's two in-house designers, Paul Blair and Patrick Chapman, had worked as a team right from the start.

Above
The Garden Bridge is Heatherwick Studio's most recent major project. Designed in collaboration with engineering consultants Arup, the bridge aims to provide a new kind of public space above the River Thames. Its elevated parkland is designed to provide both fresh views of the city and a new river crossing for pedestrians. The project was put out for public consultation in late 2013.

'Heatherwick had come with a conceptual style and stance, and it was our job to make that a reality', recalls Blair. 'They had a clear idea of what they wanted to achieve, and although there was no animosity, there were some tricky situations when we had to say that you simply couldn't do it like that.'

Exterior Design

Wrightbus's designers were enthusiastic about pushing the boundaries on a concept for a single customer, rather than producing a more standardised, off-the-shelf product to please everyone on the open market. At Heatherwick Studio, meanwhile, a rather different process was going on, with the small team trying to absorb and understand the rationale that had allowed general bus design to become so sterile. 'We had lots of questions about why buses seemed to be so un-coordinated in a design sense', remembers Wood. 'To our at that point amateur eyes, the critique that we could offer was one of a lack of coordination, a lack of sensitivity. In the commercial car world there is incredible sensitivity, incredible attention to detail. Our perception was that the bus world seemed to have become a victim of regulation and an economic commercial model that squeezed out any opportunity for anything other than the norm.'

The commission to design and build a successor to the fabled

Left
Early sketches from Heatherwick Studio show how the characteristic curves and exterior graphics of the New Routemaster were there from the very beginning.

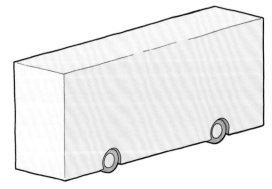

Routemaster was in direct defiance of that norm. Here was a vehicle that could be shaped around the specific needs and preferences of Londoners, just like the original of 1959; it would be sensitive and individual, not a bland pan-European design, and it would not have to be built at a rock-bottom price. Yet, contrary to the general expectation, Wood and his team were not asked to make a new Routemaster. 'In fact,' he explains, 'we weren't given any guidance of that description: we were given technical parameters, and the rest was over to us. But we did of course reference the Routemaster in many of our conversations because it was a very stylish, well-engineered, creative and memorable result. We were interested in what contributed to that, as opposed to trying to copy it.'

The technical template brought by TfL already prescribed an open rear platform for the conductor, two further entrances and twin staircases. In addition, as Mike Weston points out, London requirements insisted on a certain seating capacity and a maximum headroom of 1.8 metres (6 feet) on both the upper and the lower deck; buses built for non-London operators often have less overall height to cope with low bridges. There was also, says Weston, the more general requirement for the provision of a wheelchair bay, level access and a flat floor.

The hybrid powertrain, including the engine, batteries and associated electrical components, had already been packaged in the chassis by Wrightbus (see page 70), so Heatherwick Studio had a set of fixed points

Below and opposite, bottom
The attractive proportions of the classic Routemaster (opposite, far left) would have been spoilt if extended to the same length as the new bus. Heatherwick Studio's solution was to round off the vehicle's front and rear elevations and, by rounding off the corners when viewed from above, introduce plan shape, thus reducing the visual mass of the bus.

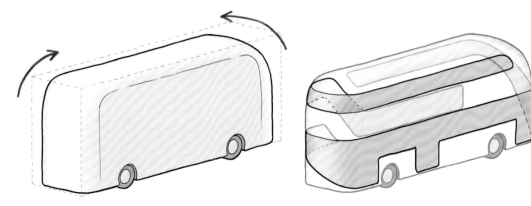

The full-scale mock-up of the new bus was built by Wrightbus at its headquarters in Ballymena and later shipped to London for testing with a wide range of user groups. The strong exterior graphics created by the contrast between the dark glazing and red paintwork are a distinctive feature.

to work around. 'Other than the bus being red, we were very much given carte blanche', says Wood. 'That was very refreshing, as we were fearful of being told to do a modern take on a classic, as with the Mini and the VW Beetle.'

Quite deliberately, Heatherwick left the envelope containing the entries from the earlier public design competitions unopened: no one wanted to be distracted by any thinking it might contain. Instead, the team decided to approach the bus as a piece of architecture; after all, reasons Wood, it has the capacity of a small building, and the cumulative effect of a lot of buses in a busy street is much like a row of buildings.

In contrast to normal cars, buses are not defined by speed or aerodynamics; instead, says Wood, they could be regarded as slow-moving buildings, in which case their design would influence not just the journey from A to B but also the experience within the bus itself. 'In the context of London and all the sights and connecting experiences it has to offer,' he explains, 'we were determined for it to be a design that had the greatest conversation with London around it – to give the best views out and the best views in. This became our mantra, and that's one of the reasons why we treated it like a piece of architecture.'

In doing so, it was natural to consider how the bus would fit in with its surroundings. A large vehicle measuring more than 11 metres (36 feet) in length, its mass had to be softened – not for aerodynamic reasons but for those of human scale. The rounding of the ends involved developing new techniques at Wrightbus for the use of load-bearing composite materials (see page 94) at the front and rear, complementing the aluminium space frame of the vehicle's centre section. Heatherwick Studio also specified strong curvatures for the substantial glass areas at either end, again setting challenges to the materials suppliers.

The story of the glass elements provides a good example of how the experience of the Wrightbus designers complemented the occasionally over-ambitious flair of their Heatherwick counterparts. The huge windscreen's complex compound curvature, for example, had to be moderated to combat night-time reflections for the driver,

Passenger flows and boarding 'dwell' times were carefully studied using architectural software and tests with real passenger groups. The use of twin staircases helps fill the upper deck more quickly.

as well as to make it less difficult to manufacture, and the original idea of having the screen descending right down to bumper level was rejected on the grounds of vulnerability to damage: 'You'd have been changing them several times a week' was one verdict. The solution was to end the windscreen just above headlight level, but to continue the distinctive diagonal line downwards with a black infill panel.

Interior

The meat of the project, says Stuart Wood, was in the 'defining and refining' of the interior: 'We were very pleased with our exterior design, but we always knew that the greatest improvement to be made was on the interior. Unquestionably, we all felt the interior design of modern buses was appalling – and I use that strong word very deliberately.'

Wood likens the interiors of buses to a collision of regulations and engineering requirements, all clustered together with no finesse and no vision. Yet the original Routemaster had a well-coordinated vision. 'Lighting was a huge component of our thinking', he continues. 'Contemporary buses have strip lights, which make the interior of the bus feel like the inside of a fridge-freezer; they make everyone look pale and ill, and everything is very over lit. We knew that if we took some of the sensitivities from the world of interior architecture – spotlights, warmer

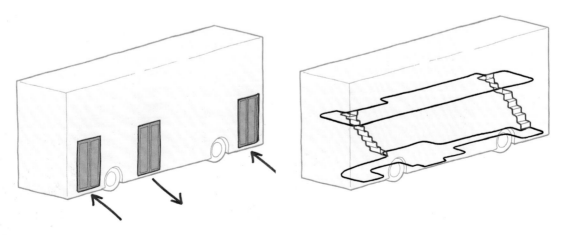

colour temperatures – we would make everyone and everything look better. In fact, we feel that one of the biggest single improvements we have made is to the lighting.'

When it came to exploring the 'touchy-feely' world of mood, colour and texture, the designers at Heatherwick brought in an additional consultant. Again, contemporary buses, with their lurid colours and plasticky textures, had shocked the team, and as in other areas of design the original Routemaster provided much of the inspiration for the interior feel of its successor. 'This is probably where we took most of our influence from the philosophy of the Routemaster,' explains Wood. 'It was very logical to have a darker lower half and a lighter ceiling.'

This palette of deep reds, creams and browns gives a warm, comforting feeling, as well as a sense of airiness, working in tandem with the carefully studied glazing. Once again following the Routemaster's example, the windows on the upper deck are relatively shallow, suiting the seated passenger and minimising solar gain while also avoiding the vulnerable, goldfish-bowl feeling of many over-glazed modern buses. Where the glazing has been especially carefully applied is in the bus's two signature graphic elements – the dramatic diagonal 'slashes' of glass denoting the staircases – which are as distinctive from the inside as they are from the outside.

The idea is for the glazing to follow the passenger, not only to his or her seat but also up the front and rear staircases. In contrast to existing double-deckers, in which the stairwells are gloomy metal tunnels, the New Routemaster has extensive glazing that tracks each of the stair routes, allowing light in and creating a greater sense of security for

Neil Hubbard, a member of the Heatherwick Studio design team, tries out the upper deck's rearmost seating position at the launch of the mock-up in November 2011.

No Detail Is Above Thoroughness

Stuart Wood led the New Bus for London team at the project's design consultants, Heatherwick Studio

'The interior was without a shadow of a doubt the toughest task. The biggest challenge was trying to keep the interior simple and trying to execute details that didn't feel compromised or forced. When I reflect on the interior, it was a total effort, and the constant focus was on trying to keep clarity and not to let ugly detail and over-complication creep in.

'It was a constant struggle to meet the provision for durability and compliance while keeping a vision. So we had to lobby hard and work hard to think on our feet and do many, many options and revisions. Many revisions, huge amounts – I would use the word exhaustive.

'It's comparable to all of our [public building] projects in the sense that we don't consider any detail to be above thoroughness; we studied the bell push and went through twenty-plus iterations.'

the passenger. This feeling is particularly dramatic at the rear, where the spiral staircase turns upwards and the passenger gains a sweeping panorama of the street as he or she climbs to the top deck.

The stair glazing serves two further purposes. In addition to providing the spectacular diagonally ascending slabs of glass that distinguish the rear and the right flank of the bus (and which have been registered internationally as a protected design), it openly advertises the bus's novel interior to passers-by, thus removing some of the barriers between passenger and pedestrian.

The Details that Count

Unlikely as it may seem, the bus's two staircases are home to several of the vehicle's most exquisite details – beautifully thought-through fixtures and fittings that, although mundane in their function, are attractive to the eye and pleasingly tactile in use, thus raising the experience of bus travel above its familiar and depressing baseline.

The spiral staircase is a nod to the elegantly curved open staircase on the rear of the NS and original LT buses of the 1920s and 1930s. Each stair tread is covered with an appealing cork/rubber material known as Treadmaster. Manufactured in Cornwall, Treadmaster is commonly used as non-slip decking on luxury yachts; on the New Routemaster, it is attractively patterned with grooves, both on the tread itself and on the riser, where people are likely to kick. Each step edge is elegantly trimmed with a bright metal finisher, which blends smoothly into the wall to integrate the steps with the interior. Every single one of these finishers is different, requiring individual three-axis machining. 'The cost is considerable,' says David Hampson-Ghani, 'but it is crucial to the design to create this feeling of a grand entrance.'

Prototype bench seats on the full-size mock-up were used to trial shapes, spacings and fabric patterns. The final choice of dark reds and greys was influenced by the colour palette of the original Routemaster.

Treadmaster, likewise, is expensive and heavy, forcing the designers to make weight savings elsewhere in the vehicle. Yet its use in the entrance areas, on the luggage shelf and on the open rear platform – where it has been given a smart fan-shaped groove pattern to facilitate wet-weather drainage – is distinctive and classy and provides a suitably up-market welcome for people entering the bus.

Seats, handrails and poles were also areas of contention, with the designers having to lobby hard to achieve the consistently high quality to which they aspired. Regulations stipulate that handrails and poles have to be at least 38 millimetres (1 ½ inches) in diameter; they do not, however, insist on the lurid yellow or lime-green colours found on most buses, merely stating that the fittings must be in a 'contrasting' finish. Stuart Wood wanted the elegance of slender, unpainted brass or bronze poles, but a compromise was found with a bronze finish on the thicker type of pole, reducing its visual prominence. Mention should also be made of the wireless bell pushes: these are one of the few parts of the bus to which Heatherwick Studio, rather than TfL, holds the rights, reflecting Wood's self-confessed obsession with the look and feel of every component, no matter how small. The bell-push design went through 'at least twenty' iterations before Wood was satisfied.

The seating on most buses is also a commodity item, and the Heatherwick team was fiercely critical of its cheap-feeling pseudo rally-seat shaping and plasticky surrounds. On a practical level, this type of seat is not only isolating for the passenger but also the perfect place to stuff litter and waste packaging, thus making life harder for the cleaning teams at the end of the bus's shift. Heatherwick fought hard for a return to Routemaster-style bench seats, together with bespoke fabric patterns in a deep-red palette and chrome frames. As in the case of the step finishers, each seat is slightly different, making them not only more

A point of pride for the design team at Heatherwick is the elegantly crafted bell push, which went through some twenty iterations before approval. Hand poles have a metallic bronze finish, rather than the yellow of other buses.

The rear staircase (above, left and right) is designed to give the feeling of a grand entrance; each stair tread, riser and metal finishing strip is individually shaped and cut. The intricately patterned flooring material is Treadmaster, normally found on boat decks, but also used to good effect on the original Routemaster. The upper saloon (left) has shallow windows to minimise the build up of heat in the summer, while individual LED lighting for each passenger provides a warm ambience at night.

At Heatherwick Studio, a test subject tries out a seating buck to evaluate the position, profile and clearances of the headliner, the material covering the inside of the roof.

expensive but also more complex when it comes to the warehousing of spare parts.

One area where Heatherwick's ambitious ideas for interior decor were considered to have gone a step too far was in the randomly rippled composite mouldings envisaged for such interior surfaces as covings. These would have created a three-dimensional look similar to that of ruched leather, but they would have been fearsomely expensive. Moreover, both TfL and Wrightbus were concerned that the material would not stand up to the rigours of an intense 18-hour working day, seven days a week. Instead, a lightly textured dark-red composite with a satin finish was selected.

Full-Scale Mock-Up

Both vehicle designers and architects tend to use CAD (computer-aided design) software, which can produce extremely realistic renderings of exterior surfaces and even allow the user to 'walk through' a virtual interior to assess sightlines and views. Yet however clever the program, when it comes to gauging the actual look and feel of a project, there is no substitute for a physical scale model. In the case of the New Routemaster, where passenger flows and such features as disabled access and handrail positioning had to be determined, the model was taken an unusual step further and became a full-scale mock-up. 'This was our most complete mock-up ever, the full vehicle', recalls Patrick Chapman, a member of the design team at Wrightbus, where the model was built. 'It was a good learning point for things we hadn't done before, like the spiral staircase and how it felt to walk up the stairs and under the domed roof. It also helped us get the lighting and the handrail positioning right.'

Above
Thomas Heatherwick
discusses the finer
points of bus design with
Dr William Wright – one
of the founders of the
family-owned Wrightbus
organisation – at an event
in November 2010.

Back in London, Stuart Wood found that the full-sized mock-up gave a completely different perception of space and depth, with many of the clearances now feeling too tight. As a result, the rear staircase dimensions were fine-tuned and head height under the roof section was increased. The model was also used to test out access for the elderly, people with restricted mobility, wheelchair users and parents with pushchairs; feedback from these user groups led to the repositioning of several of the poles and also a more accessible location for one of the Oyster-card readers. Lighting, too, could now be tested, important in view of the switch to LED spotlights with a much warmer colour temperature than the traditional strip lights.

While the Heatherwick and Wrightbus design teams were finalising their exterior and interior treatments in parallel, a much larger team of skilled engineers, also at Wrightbus, was developing the bus's chassis, with its sophisticated hybrid powertrain packaging. As the next chapter reveals, it was also finding ingenious ways to adapt Wrightbus's familiar construction processes in order to accommodate the novel features demanded by Heatherwick's body design.

Left and opposite
For the all-important
presentation to Mayor
Boris Johnson in April
2010, Heatherwick
Studio created a series of
highly realistic computer
renderings of the new
bus in action. St Paul's
Cathedral was just one
of the iconic locations
used as backgrounds.

Pushing the Boundaries

Paul Blair and Patrick Chapman were members of the Wrightbus team that worked on the New Routemaster

Blair 'Having a single customer in this whole process definitely helped: we normally have to design for everyone. It was a truly unique brief, once we got to that phase, and that made the whole thing stand out.

'London is unique: when you have one customer and you've got the numbers to make the bus a commercially viable product, then you can tailor the product exactly to that customer's needs. We don't normally have that luxury, and for the foreseeable future I think we will continue with a number of customers having to be satisfied. However, we do still pay a lot of attention to details: we even take into account how the bus will be cleaned.'

Chapman 'The New Routemaster is very bespoke, but it has certainly given us a great opportunity to show what can be done when you embrace design and materials and the actual feel of the interior. Many operators put their brand at the forefront of what they want their bus to say, rather than thinking about the passenger experience. The passenger's experience was always the drive behind the New Routemaster – new lighting, new materials, a more welcoming environment.'

5

The Engineering

Pages 88–89
In bus design, CAD models allow engineers to explore different solutions and stylists to view different angles. Here, the new bus is shown in its entirety, with the rear as a wireframe and the front with surface rendering to give an impression of the final product.

When it came to the tendering process and securing from TfL the order for the New Routemaster, Wrightbus was in a strong position. It had been supplying buses for use in London since the 1980s, and so was fully aware of the way in which the organisation worked; in addition, it had already built many different double-decker buses on chassis supplied by Volvo and other manufacturers. But it was only after securing the contract – which at that stage was limited to the design and development of the new bus, plus the construction of six prototypes for evaluation – and digesting the detail of its demands that the engineers at the company's Ballymena headquarters were able to appreciate the very different nature of the challenge they were facing.

First of all, TfL's environmental requirements were among the strictest yet seen in the bus industry, as David Hampson-Ghani remembers: 'We took the performance of the best hybrids then available [in 2009] and stretched it – quite a lot.' So it was that Wrightbus duly received a set of specifications for fuel consumption and the emission of carbon dioxide, carbon monoxide, hydrocarbons, nitrogen oxides and particulate matter that were well ahead of the then prevailing Euro V standards for commercial vehicles. According to David

Wrightbus designer Patrick Chapman works on the front portion of the bus, including the forward entrance, the driver's cab and its protective screen.

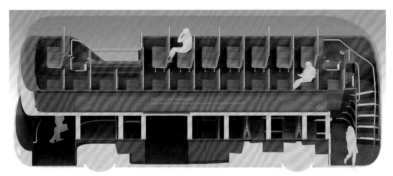

CAD visualisations from Heatherwick Studio allowed Wrightbus designers to fine-tune passenger flows, seat pitch and headroom. The dome above the rear staircase proved to be one of the most difficult areas to design.

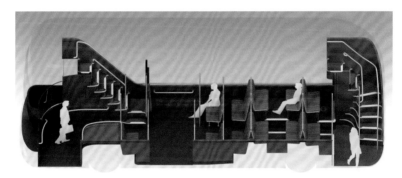

Barnett, at that stage engineering development manager at Wrightbus, it soon became clear that existing hybrid solutions would not be up to the task, and that a new type of powertrain would be required.

Equally pressing was TfL's stipulation that the design of the new bus should incorporate two staircases and three doors, one of which could be used to close off the open rear platform so cherished by the project's greatest champion, Mayor Boris Johnson. In standard-format double-deckers, the engines are generally placed transversely across the very rear of the bus, while the floor line within the bus usually rises gradually towards the rear so as to make space for the rear axle, gearbox and other parts. But with the TfL requirements dictating a low-level 'hop-on, hop-off' platform at the rear, as well as a rear staircase, this conventional arrangement would no longer work. Wrightbus had to find somewhere else, somewhere very clever, to package not only the bulky, hot and noisy engine but also all the other driveline components. 'We

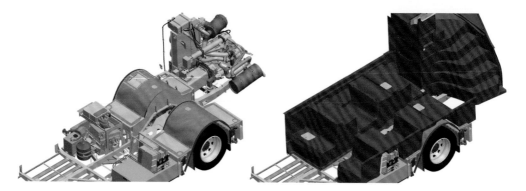

An engineering layout of the rear chassis area clearly shows the engine and emissions-control equipment at the back, with the drive motor, control electronics and traction battery just forward of the rear wheels. The composite stair assembly (in red) neatly encapsulates all the driveline components.

CAD visualisations allow designers to rotate the model around any chosen axis, as well as to see through the outer skin to the structure and engineering components beneath.

knew fairly early on that such requirements as the miles-per-gallon figure would mean going for a series hybrid', explains Barnett. 'There was no other way you could meet them – and in any case, the format of the bus would make it difficult to fit in a conventional hybrid.'

A conventional hybrid consists of a large diesel engine and a comparatively small electric motor, which provides some drive assistance and helps to recuperate energy when the bus is slowing down. A series hybrid, by contrast, is composed of a more powerful electric motor and a smaller diesel engine, the main purpose of which is to keep the electric motor's battery charged via a generator; the bus itself is driven entirely by the electric motor, which is positioned close to the rear wheels. A further advantage of the series-hybrid powertrain is that its constituent elements can to some extent be split up and placed at convenient locations within the vehicle's chassis.

Wrightbus's ingenious solution to the problem posed by the New Routemaster's layout was to place the diesel engine – a comparatively small four-cylinder unit – longitudinally in the rear right-hand corner of the bus, where it could be hidden under the staircase. The substantial batteries would be positioned just ahead of the left-hand rear wheels, under the seats, while the drive motor and electronics would occupy

The four-cylinder Cummins engine is cantilevered off the rear of the chassis. It drives a generator to charge the main battery, which then powers the traction motor. The engine runs only when the battery needs topping up, saving fuel and making for quieter travel.

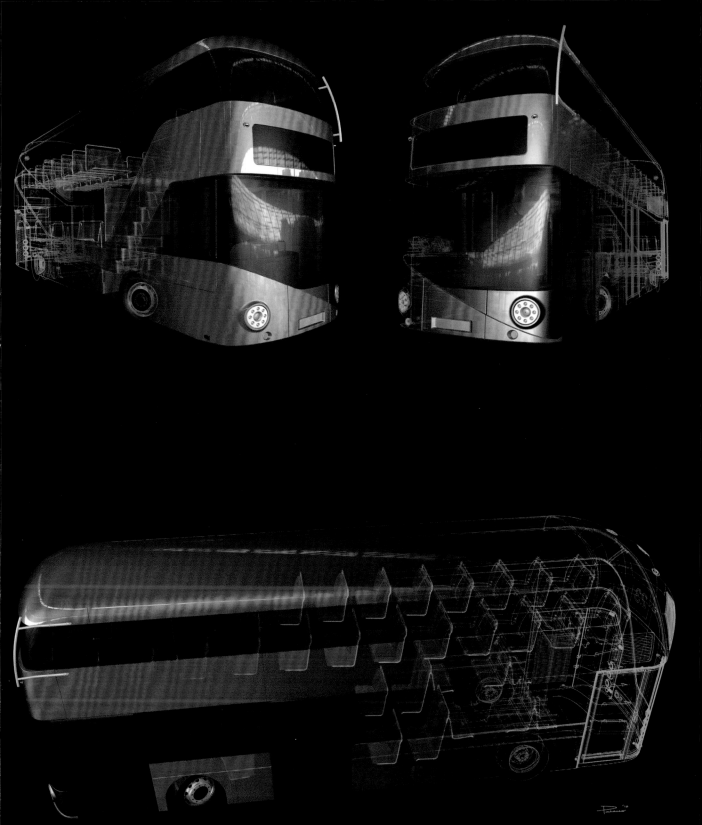

a similar space on the right-hand side. Having arrived at such a solution, however, Wrightbus was faced with a further challenge: in contrast to the standard practice of the day, there was no existing powertrain or chassis that it could turn to. 'Our constraints were very tight', says Barnett. 'On some of our previous hybrids, we have basically bought the chassis and engine. But in this case we had to start with a completely new layout and re-evaluate all the component choices.'

The largely tailor-made chassis incorporates an electric motor by Siemens, batteries by Valence, a DC–DC converter from US Hybrid and a 4.4-litre diesel engine by Cummins. 'The basic engine is reasonably off-the-shelf,' explains Barnett, 'but the control of it is very much bespoke to us, to suit the series application.' In series-hybrid operation, the diesel engine starts up only when the battery needs recharging; it will then run at its most efficient speed until the battery is topped up. Only in an emergency, when the battery is flat, will the engine power the electric motor directly.

Big Decisions: Engineering the Structure

While the powertrain engineers were busy ensuring that the innovative series-hybrid set-up met or exceeded all the performance and emissions requirements, as well as tough TfL operational demands — all of which called for intense, almost 24/7 shift patterns — Wrightbus's structural experts were having to deal with a very different issue. In order for it to be both strong and light enough not to compromise the aggressive fuel-consumption targets, the body configuration, with its three entrances, twin staircases and rounded ends, demanded a new type of construction. The solution devised by the body team was highly unorthodox, demanding a variation in Wrightbus's normal methods of construction: while the centre section and most of the front would be made of aluminium, the entire rear portion aft of the rear axle would be formed of a strong yet lightweight composite material, as employed in the making of luxury yachts and the blades of wind turbines.

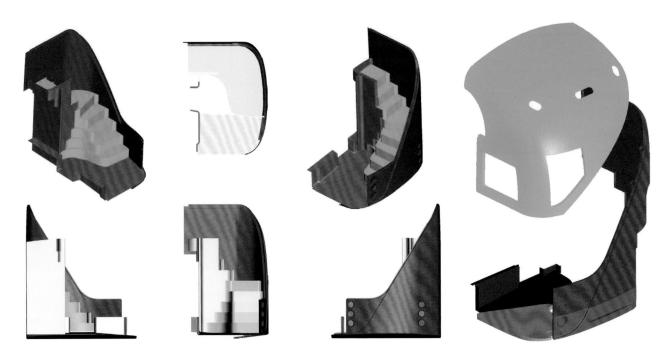

The rear dome of the bus plays a critical role in the vehicle's construction: its five structural components support the weight of the engine, the passengers on the platform, the staircase and the upper deck. Thus, according to Gurit – the composite-materials supplier with which Wrightbus collaborated closely on the project – the use of such materials 'saved several hundred kilograms from the structural weight of the bus, compared with traditional materials, and allows the bus to carry enough passengers without exceeding the legal weight limit'.

Heatherwick Studio, by its own admission, spent the majority of its time on the interior, resulting in solutions that were both innovative and aesthetically pleasing. These solutions, in turn, set up additional challenges for the Wrightbus engineers, who had to tweak the design in order to achieve certain legal stipulations, such as the amount of headroom above seats and the distances between hand poles. Lighting was another case in point. Heatherwick's preference for LED spotlights over the conventional strip lights meant a new approach to the layout, as senior design engineer Sam McCartney explains: 'Strip lights are a lot easier. In fact, it was a lot more troublesome to meet the designers' preferences than the legal requirements.'

The design of the rear-platform door, which is in two parts, one of them operated manually, provides another example of the project throwing up new challenges, in this case for both Wrightbus and the door supplier. Other such challenges, as mentioned in an earlier chapter, were the tricky glass wraparounds for the front and rear of the bus, the metallic stair edgings and the composite trim mouldings inside the upper and lower cabin areas.

Wrightbus's CAD visualisations of the rear of the bus show the construction of the stairwell and the complex shapes of the load-bearing composite shell (in red) and floor (in lilac).

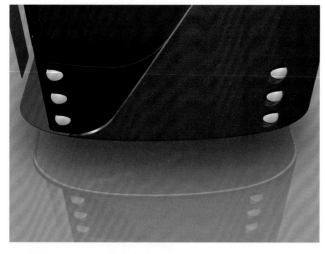

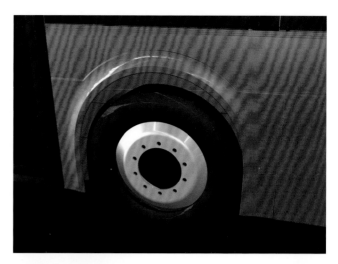

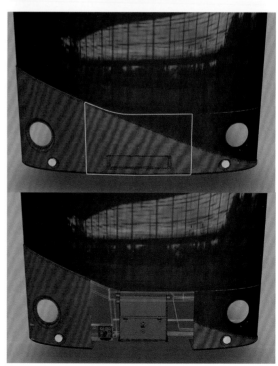

Opposite
Computer renderings of selected components and systems, including the rear staircase, the distinctive headlight bezel and the front of the bus with and without the service access panel in place.

Cab Design and Drivers' Views

The design of the driver's cab was another area that revealed contrasting approaches from Heatherwick, Wrightbus and TfL. At Heatherwick, Stuart Wood was conscious of the need to give the driver both comfort and security: 'The driver's cab is one of the most sensitive areas. We gave it lots of attention to make it the best workplace it could be, but also making the drivers feel protected. Yet it was also important that they didn't feel restricted while driving.' Many consultations later, with TfL, test drivers and union representatives having tried out the new cab arrangement on the bus mock-up, the design was finalised. It now incorporated a revised safety screen clamped into curved frames top and bottom. 'It took a fair bit of guidance,' admits McCartney, 'but it was worth it in the end. The drivers are very pleased with the set-up.'

Part of the cab-testing process involved manoeuvring the test vehicle into Wrightbus's paint shop, which had been specially blacked out. Wrightbus workers then shone torches into the bus, from all angles and directions, to determine and eliminate internal reflections that could distract the driver at night. This, says Paul Blair, is one of the most important considerations when designing a bus cab.

As in the case of any vehicle designed for intense public service over a working life of at least fifteen years, New Routemaster prototypes were put through exhaustive durability tests. These were carried out

Above
The wooden mock-up (left) begins to take shape in the summer of 2010. The prototype cab (right) was trialled with drivers' groups and union reps; in-service buses have a protective screen fitted across the entrance.

Early prototypes undergo testing at Millbrook Proving Ground in May 2011. The main purpose of the tests was to check the structural integrity of the chassis and body, and to develop the powertrain and software. The front stairwell windows were blacked out to hide the non-final stairs, while a black mask was used to shield the prototype dashboard assembly.

on special rigs, at such specialised proving grounds as Millbrook in Bedfordshire, and out on the open road. Millbrook is home to a high-speed circular track and every conceivable type of test route and surface, from mountain and city courses to steep inclines for hill starts, brake-testing areas, and roads with monstrous potholes, craters and projecting kerbs to test the suspension, steering and chassis to destruction.

Some of the most sophisticated testing went into confirming the durability of the bus's innovative composite construction. Another part of the official safety evaluation is to test the bus on a tilt table. Even with a full load on both upper and lower decks, representing some 5 tonnes of passengers, the bus must not tip over before the table has reached an angle of 28 degrees to the horizontal. Despite this apparently alarming angle of lean, the bus passed the test with ease.

A Question of Cost

Ever since Boris Johnson's 2008 mayoral election campaign, during which he first hatched the idea of putting a modern Routemaster on London's streets, the new iteration has been a political issue. Political opponents have tried to denounce it as a costly vanity project; others have criticised the way the programme was structured and the contracts drawn up. There is also the lingering suspicion among many — fuelled by often sensationalist media reports — that the bus's developers were given carte blanche to throw in high-priced materials and components merely to satisfy their artistic whims. The bottom line of all the accusations was that the new bus was a luxury we could not afford, that it would be significantly more expensive than a standard hybrid bus, and that taxpayers would be asked to fund the difference.

Indeed, with TfL agreeing to pay £11.3 million for the primary research and development contract plus six prototypes (later increased to eight), the media revelled in such headlines as 'The £2 Million Bus'. What was conveniently ignored by such reports, however, was the 'sunk'

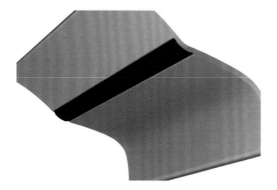
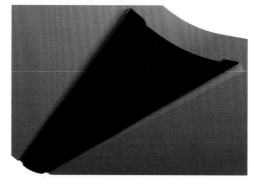

The coving mouldings between the bus sides and the headliner are typical of the details that took time and effort to resolve.

cost: the already incurred research and development cost that, when spread across the proposed production run of between 600 and 1,000 buses, helps to lower their individual cost.

Yet, with Johnson re-elected as London mayor in May 2012, and with TfL about to confirm an order for 600 production buses, the money question once again raised its head when the cost of the vehicles through to 2016 was revealed as £354,000 each. Critics were quick to point out that this was significantly more than the £300,000-odd for a standard bus, as well as vastly more than the 'under £250,000' of which the Mayor had boasted in a London Assembly exchange in 2009, as reported in *The Londonist* on 3 May 2013.

The truth, says Leon Daniels, is that there were many discussions underway about how the buses should be funded. One proposal even involved London Underground using its purchasing muscle to get the buses' motors at a favourable price. 'In the end,' says Daniels, 'I did the deal personally with Wrightbus in the old-fashioned way, glaring across the table and then shaking hands at the end when we'd got our deal.' TfL maintains that although the New Routemaster is indeed slightly more expensive than a standard hybrid bus, the gap is nowhere near as big as the critics allege. Over the term of the contract, the fixed price of

The full-size mock-up in the development bay at the Wrightbus plant in Ballymena.

NEWS

£354,500 each: The price of a NBfL

Fixed-price contract "to save millions and remove risk" says TfL

By Mel Holley

Transport for London (TfL) has revealed details of the £212.7m contract it has signed with Wrightbus to supply 600 New Bus for London (NBfL) double-deckers over the next six years.

TfL says that it has agreed a fixed-price contract with Wrightbus that "bears down

comparable with a standard hybrid double deck bus."

It adds: " The price difference is accounted for by the much higher specification of the new bus compared to a standard hybrid bus. The new bus boasts a number of additional design features, including the innovative three-door, two-staircase design which allows quicker boarding and alighting at bus stops, helping to reduce overall journey times."

TfL also claims that NBfL is the "greenest diesel electric hybrid bus in the world" producing "around four times less of the PM and NOx of the fleet average hybrid bus and 20% less CO2."

Wrightbus-built NBfL to be in London service until at least 2030

be delivered over the useful life of the buses, even taking into

the capital to operate entirely with NBfL. The route operated

May 2013: *RouteOne* magazine reports TfL's announcement that the fixed-price contract with Wrightbus would 'save millions and remove risk'.

£354,000 translates as £326,000 at 2013 prices, just £26,000 more than an off-the-shelf model.

Whatever the final figure, there can be no doubt that this is not a bus built down to a rock-bottom price. Almost everything inside the bus comes with a certain premium because it has been custom-made for the project: the seats, the lighting, the flooring, the stairs and the stair rails, which even Hampson-Ghani admits were 'considerable in terms of cost'. Another source has conceded that these items have added 'thousands of pounds to the cost of each bus'.

Stuart Wood denies any wanton largesse, however, saying that, in close collaboration with Wrightbus, Heatherwick kept a keen eye on costs in order to achieve the best possible result within the agreed limits. 'For sure, [the bus] had a higher anticipated final cost than a so-called normal hybrid bus. That was the premium for the open platform and the second staircase. But it still had an upper boundary.' Wherever possible, adds Wood, a cost over-run on one component was offset by a saving somewhere else. 'But to do something new,' he says, 'to do something special, comes with an extra cost — and it's just about how much that extra cost is.'

From the Driver's Seat

For a bus to be judged truly successful, it must please not only its owners and operators (an assessment that generally comes down to value for money) but also its passengers and drivers, which is where the experience of riding on the bus comes in. And if everybody else who interacts with the vehicle likes it too, then better still.

It is of course early days for the New Routemaster, but the initial signs are that the bus has already scored a big hit with the public. Passers-by point and stare, tourists pose in front of it for photographs, and evidence from TfL suggests that, on the routes it serves, passenger numbers have increased since it came into service — not only because the three doors allow greater numbers to get on and off in a given time,

The complex, computer-milled foam model from which the mould for the rear stair assembly was made. The final composite structure helps support the upper deck.

but also because many people actually prefer the smooth, classy ride it offers and actively seek it out for their journeys.Indeed, according to Leon Daniels, TfL is withdrawing Heritage Routemasters from route 9 because the New Routemasters operating on the same service are proving so popular.

Pedestrians, too, prefer the New Routemaster, because a lot of its operation is accomplished under near-silent electric power, rather than the smoky and smelly clatter of a diesel engine. There is little to hear, for instance, as the bus pulls away from a bus stop save for the remote whirr of its electric motor. London's West End, for one, would be a much quieter place if all its buses were New Routemasters.

It is, however, the people who use the bus most, spending seven or eight hours a day on board, who are among its greatest admirers. Ravi Raval, who has been a London bus driver for twenty-eight years and has driven 'every route and every type of bus', says that the New Routemaster is his first choice on the fleet – apart from the original Routemaster. 'The LT [the new bus's official designation] has smooth steering and braking,' he explains, 'and there's no need to think about gears. The visibility is excellent, as we have to put public safety first and look out for cyclists, pedestrians and motorcyclists.' Having driven the New Routemaster on route 24 (Pimlico to Hampstead Heath) 'ever since it came out', Raval is very comfortable with the stop and start of the engine, and is enthusiastic about the responsiveness of the electric drive. Conductors are a brilliant idea too, he says, while passengers love the bus so much that they want to be photographed with it.

Martin Bennett's London-bus-driving record goes back an astonishing forty-five years, during which time he has driven 'everything London Transport has ever had, from the RT [the predecessor to the original Routemaster] to the latest LT. I've even driven the RTW [a wider version of the RT] on the skid pan.' Bennett rates the New Routemaster as 'easier, and cushier' than any other bus type. When driving a bus, Bennett pays particular attention to applying the brakes smoothly in order to give the passengers a comfortable ride. Here, the new bus

James May and the team from *Top Gear* put the new bus through its paces in Weston-super-Mare, Somerset, in May 2013 – entertaining the locals in the process.

performs much better than other bus types, on which the intervention of the retarder (a mechanism used in conjunction with the primary braking system) can sometimes lead to jerky travel. 'The light steering makes life easier,' adds Bennett, 'and having just the one gear makes it smoother too.' The RT, he remembers, had a preselector gearbox, and the driver had to rev the engine every time he changed down a gear.

Bennett admits that the electric powertrain 'felt strange at first', but says that, in comparison with other hybrid and conventional buses, the New Routemaster is never at a disadvantage in terms of acceleration or hill climbing. In common with Raval, Bennett values the presence of the conductor, particularly when it comes to assisting with the boarding of wheelchair passengers. In fact, he adds, boarding in general is noticeably quicker – as long as the passengers realise that they can board through any of the three doors. 'Passengers really like [the bus], and people on the pavement point and give me the thumbs-up signal. I've driven lots of different London buses, but the new LT is my favourite.'

There is equal enthusiasm for the New Routemaster at Bennett and Raval's Holloway bus garage, which is run by Metroline. Operations support manager Stuart McManus says that the vehicle is easier to clean than other bus types, partly because there is more legroom between the seats. He does point out, however, that there is more glass involved, which means that the bus takes longer to clean. McManus also confirms TfL's initial observation that the new bus has experienced less vandalism, with passengers appearing to respect it much more than the other buses in the fleet.

So high is the public profile of the New Routemaster that it has even made it into the mainstream motoring magazines. Following on from its Routemaster reinvention design study in December 2007, *Autocar* made the final product the subject of its special Christmas road test four years later. The magazine's hard-driving testers, more used to a diet of high-performance supercars than slow-moving public transport, praised the New Routemaster's smooth power delivery, slick and consistently light steering, and admirable ironing-out of imperfections in the road

The leading members of the New Routemaster team pose alongside, and on the platform of, the prototype. From left to right are Mike Weston, David Barnett, David Hampson-Ghani, Stuart Wood, Neil Hubbard, Patrick Chapman and Thomas Heatherwick.

surface. 'The capital's first new bus for fifty years is as postcard-friendly as it's possible to get', ran the review. 'More significantly, though, the [New Routemaster] is a triumph of product design in an otherwise utterly unengaging and unromantic market.' What seals the bus's five-star rating, concluded the testers, 'is that it's as advanced under the body as it is interesting inside it. Clean, efficient and thought-provoking, it's public transport as it should be.'

In the summer of 2013, the new bus also found its way on to the small screen when it made an appearance on *Top Gear*, the BBC's flagship and internationally watched motoring programme. Presenter James May, always a strong supporter of unusual forms of transport, braved the taunts of his speed-loving fellow presenters and took the bus for a drive in the Somerset countryside. His itinerary included the stately home of Longleat House and the picturesque village of Castle Combe, where May managed to manoeuvre the bus in a very tight space – to the obvious amusement of the villagers.

The non-specialist media were also eager to comment on the bus in service, generally in positive terms, but sometimes with a degree of lingering political sniping. Yet the most voluble enthusiast remains the man whose energy catalysed the whole project. 'The look and the emotional appeal of the New Routemaster of course owes a lot to its predecessor', said Mayor Boris Johnson when questioned for this book. 'But now its reinterpretation by the great Thomas Heatherwick has thrust this icon of London transport firmly into the twenty-first century. Londoners always looked on the original Routemaster with fond eyes', he continued. 'They saw it as something that was synonymous with the hustle and bustle of our city. The new version has distilled everything that was great about the old, and I think that people recognise that. They see a beautifully designed piece of modern engineering that is in some way doffing its conductor's hat to a distant cousin.'

Building the Mock-Up

The New Routemaster broke so much new ground in bus design that Wrightbus decided to build a full-scale mock-up – the first time it had ever taken such a step. The mock-up, made of a variety of materials, including plywood, MDF and glass fibre, gave the designers and users valuable insights into how the bus's novel layout would operate in practice. Seen here are the interior of the rear dome, the stair and floor construction, and the overall frame structure.

Inside the Mock-Up

The driver's cab area (below) was the subject of special attention, with the design team determined to improve ergonomics, comfort and visual harmomy. The mock-up proved invaluable in finalising the specification and location of such key details as hand rails and poles; many changes were made as a result of user-group trials.

The First Prototype

Designated LT1, the first prototype New Routemaster (opposite, below right and bottom) has its surfaces readied and its glass masked as it prepares to go into the paint booth at Wrightbus's Ballymena plant. At this stage in the development of the bus, a second prototype is already under construction (below left).

Planning the Production Line

An indicative production line is set up at Wrightbus's Ballymena plant in November 2011 prior to Boris Johnson's visit. The black paint finish on the chassis (below) will later be augmented by a blue powder coating for series-production examples. Clearly visible in the buses under construction are the series-hybrid electrical system (below, centre left), the engine (below, centre right) and the complex systems behind the driver's cab (opposite, top right).

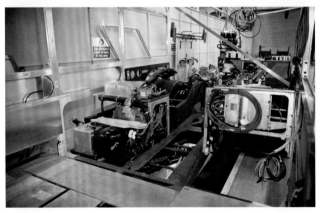

The Chassis Plant

May 2013: the brand-new assembly hall at the Wrightbus factory is opened by Boris Johnson. Here, New Routemasters share the space with engine-less chassis for the smaller StreetLite model (below, foreground). Elsewhere in the hall, Routemaster chassis undergo final assembly (opposite, top and bottom), including the fitting of the power steering and the testing of the pneumatic circuits. Yellow and red bands indicate 'assembly' and 'clear' zones respectively.

The Assembly Line

This is the last stage of the assembly line before the bus is commissioned and driven off. The vehicles are raised to provide access to components on the underside. The software systems are loaded up, the communication modules are checked, and the bus can be started up and driven for the first time.

Opposite, bottom right
One of the two main
assembly lines, which
together produce six New
Routemasters a week.

Above
The commissioning
bay seen from the rear,
with two buses raised
to provide access to
chassis systems.

Right
Four completed New
Routemasters and
other finished buses await
shipment to operators.
In the foreground is one
of the New Routemaster
assembly lines.

The New Routemaster

The Mock-Up Goes on Show, 10 November 2010

The full-size mock-up of the New Routemaster arrives in London for the first time. Here, it is being prepared at London Transport Museum's Acton depot for the press presentation with Boris Johnson planned for the following day; the ceremony will include two minutes' silence for Armistice Day. In March 2011 the mock-up was put on display at the museum's Covent Garden site, where it was exhibited alongside a classic Routemaster and older double-deckers.

Pages 120–21
16 August 2012: London's New Routemaster poses for a publicity shot on Westminster Bridge.

4 November 2011

The launch of LT1, the first New Routemaster off the prototype production line. At the wheel is London Mayor Boris Johnson, who drove around the Wrightbus factory after receiving some special tuition for the occasion. 'This is a world-class piece of technology, built here in Ballymena', he declared. 'It's the most amazing, futuristic design, but it's also the cleanest, greenest bus that will ply the streets of London, indeed any city in the UK.'

The New Routemaster Arrives in London, 16 December 2011

Parked on the piazza outside City Hall on London's South Bank, the New Routemaster cuts a fine figure in the rain. Later the same day, Leon Daniels drove the bus to Westminster Bridge, where Sir Peter Hendy took over for the final leg to Trafalgar Square and the bus's official London launch.

Entering Passenger Service, 27 February 2012

The New Routemaster takes its first fare-paying passengers on route 38 (Clapton Pond to Victoria Bus Station). The level of public interest is obvious from the number of onlookers and bus enthusiasts who turn up to witness and photograph the occasion. Delivered just two days before, this was the second vehicle off the assembly line.

The New Routemaster in Service

Drivers, conductors and passengers aboard a selection of operational New Routemasters. On show are the welcoming ambience of the interior and the easy access for wheelchair users via the built-in boarding ramp.

Fresh off the Assembly Line

The first eight New Routemaster working prototypes are pictured at bus operator Arriva's Ash Grove depot in Hackney, east London. The buses' crews (right) were hand-picked from the many drivers who volunteered to work on the new bus. As with any new bus type, they were given a half-day's conversion training.

The New Routemaster
continues its tour of
London landmarks as
Wrightbus completes
the vehicle's portfolio of
publicity pictures. Later,
two of the buses would
extend this exercise to
other major cities
worldwide as part of a
global promotional tour
(see pages 140–41).

Pages 136–37
Two London landmarks:
the new bus negotiates
Trafalgar Square on its
photographic tour of the
West End.

The First Production Buses Leave the Factory, March 2013

Destined for service on route 24 (Grosvenor Road to Royal Free Hospital), which is run by Metroline, the first three full-production buses leave the Ballymena plant for the docks and London. The convoy took the Belfast–Liverpool crossing and then drove straight to the capital. The previous eight examples, serving on route 38 (see pages 132–33), were part of the original TfL order for design, development and prototype buses.

GREAT Bus Tour

Just as the first series-production buses were entering service in London, the first prototype was being readied at the Wrightbus factory for a strictly confidential mission of great importance. It was to be the elegant spearhead of the British government's 'GREAT Britain' campaign, an international marketing initiative designed not only to show off the very best of what Britain has to offer, but also to encourage the world to visit, study and do business with the United Kingdom.

Linking the promotional efforts of the Foreign and Commonwealth Office (FCO), UK Trade and Investment, the Department for Culture, Media and Sport, VisitBritain, and the British Council, GREAT's first stop was New York. The bus was shipped there amid much secrecy on 9 May 2013, and, thanks to extensive cooperation from the city and state authorities, it was allowed to begin a series of test runs and be used for driver training. This despite the fact that it did not comply with local regulations, especially when it came to height.

'A red London bus is again gracing the streets of New York', said an excited Leon Daniels in his account of the trip. 'A New Routemaster is today travelling along the streets of Manhattan as it undertakes a special assignment, conveying

NEW YORK, MAY 2013

COLOMBIA, JULY 2013

SOUTH KOREA, OCTOBER 2013

HRH Prince Harry and Prime Minister David Cameron to a major event promoting British innovation and technology.' For Wrightbus, David Barnett commented: 'We have been delighted by the New Routemaster project, and it has been thrilling to see it attract so much attention around the world. Quite literally, the New Routemasters have stopped traffic wherever they've gone.' The GREAT tour, he added, has given both Wrightbus and TfL the opportunity to show what can be achieved with a shared vision and a commitment to deliver.

In conjunction with Wrightbus and TfL, the promotional buses — now two in number — continued on their worldwide tour, taking in Colombia, South Korea, Poland, Austria, Turkey, Hong Kong, Malaysia, Bahrain and Singapore. The GREAT-branded buses have criss-crossed the globe by land and sea, and have been visited by representatives of many of the world's leading companies, foreign and UK government ministers, dignitaries, the Mayor of London, fashion designers, models — and even celebrity chefs. They have also been seen by hundreds of thousands of members of the general public, and have been a showcase for UK excellence in green technology, infrastructure, retail, food and drink, education, and financial services.

TURKEY, NOVEMBER 2013

BAHRAIN, JANUARY 2014

SINGAPORE, FEBRUARY 2014

THE NEW ROUTEMASTER

7

The Future

When it comes to believing that your own city is special, Londoners do so with a rare passion. Historically, as the first million-person metropolis in the Western world, London was forced by its sheer size to invent many of the essential systems, from an underground rail network to double-deckers and traffic lights, that enable large urban expanses to operate effectively, and which have subsequently come to define mature cities around the world. For Londoners, these inventions are a source of some pride, none more so than the big red double-decker bus, as much a symbol of the capital as Big Ben or Buckingham Palace.

The power of transport systems to characterise the cities they serve is undeniable: just think of New York and its yellow cabs, Vienna and its trams, San Francisco and its cable cars, and Venice with its gondolas and *vaporetti*. And now, with the arrival of the New Routemaster, London's globally visible transport icon has been updated for the new century. One of its tasks will be to help undo the image of London as a retro-flavoured city and reshape it into something much more excitingly futuristic.

When asked if his team at Heatherwick Studio set out to produce an iconic design, as proclaimed at every opportunity by the bus's champion, Mayor Boris Johnson, Stuart Wood resists a simplistic answer: 'We're all very nervous about the word "iconic", because if somebody asks you to produce an icon, it's almost the kiss of death. Whether or not something is iconic is completely out of our hands, but what we were very aware of was that we were treading in the footsteps of an icon: the Routemaster.'

Yet, rather than merely trying to imitate the Routemaster, Wood and his team sought to get behind what had made it iconic. 'For most people,' he continues, 'what made it iconic was its simplicity, its clarity and its specificity — it is an incredibly specific design. So we took those characteristics to heart, and the rest is about hoping that people will come to find it iconic.'

It cannot be overlooked, either, that the original Routemaster was a political product, conceived to fulfil the economic needs of the late 1950s as the swelling population of Greater London sought affordable

A New Routemaster sports a special silver paint job in honour of the 'Year of the Bus' campaign. Running throughout 2014, and intended to reconnect Londoners with their bus network and remind the world of the bus's importance to the city, the campaign will include a series of special events in and around the capital.

mobility to access new opportunities in education, employment and leisure. It was the product of an enlightened and centralised organisation – London Transport – that had the breadth of vision to know what was needed, and the financial clout to ensure that the vision became a reality. And, perhaps most crucially of all, it was first proposed in the early 1950s, at the height of a bus boom, by designers who were at the top of their game, ensuring that it would last a great deal longer than even they could have imagined.

The conclusion is unavoidable: buses are at their best when operators and manufacturers work together, when the broader view is able to prevail over the treatment of the bus as a commodity, and when quality of design and materials is allowed to take precedence over a focus purely on initial purchase price in a free-for-all market.

The Business Case

More than five decades have elapsed since the original Routemaster first turned a wheel, and many of those decades have been bleak ones for the bus business, with some politicians openly undermining the status of bus travel. More recently, however, beginning with the return of a London mayor in 2000, investment in buses has picked up and coordinated planning has become more important. The New Routemaster marks another important step in the move towards a truly modern bus network that is appropriate for London. Like its predecessor, it is a strategic product, centrally conceived with the interests of Londoners in mind, rather than simply being what the manufacturers happened to provide; also like the Routemaster, it has succeeded in rising above the run-of-the-mill, providing a premium experience that raises the quality threshold for bus travel in a major city.

Subtle changes in the business model behind the New Routemaster signal further moves towards a clear future-oriented policy. Instead of commercially leasing the New Routemaster, as they do with other buses, operating companies simply pay TfL a symbolic annual lease of £1; TfL buys the buses outright, having exploited the clout of its £200 million-plus budget to negotiate a good price for the 600-bus order that followed Boris Johnson's second victory in the contest to become London's mayor.

David Hampson-Ghani explains that since the initial batch of 600 buses are intended to remain in TfL service for the whole of their operational life, outright ownership is the most financially effective arrangement. Accountancy rules also point towards the new buses counting as restricted assets, since they would not be suitable for use outside London. This means that they must stay on TfL's books, irrespective of the lease arrangements with the operators. 'The operators normally buy or lease,' adds Mike Weston, 'and they recover their costs through the contract price. So there's no real difference with the new arrangement – and it also reduces the risk for the operators.' All the operators are very keen to run the new bus, he says. 'In practice, they all want to be involved.'

Looking Ahead

By the time the last of the initial batch of 600 production buses has entered service in April 2016, many key changes will have been incorporated into the bus's design to improve its performance. Wrightbus is already working on an engineering package that will bring the bus into line with the next round of European emissions standards, Euro VI. Each new round normally carries a fuel-consumption penalty, so the engineers will have to build in a significant weight reduction to offset that penalty and enable the bus to return to where it started in terms of CO_2 emissions.

Two distinguished passengers try out a New Routemaster for size. The occasion was Their Royal Highnesses' official visit to the Wrightbus plant in Ballymena in June 2013. Prince Charles took the opportunity to present Wrightbus co-founder Dr William Wright with a lifetime achievement award.

More immediately, TfL and Wrightbus are investigating the initially disappointing fuel-consumption returns of the buses currently in service. The bus industry does not yet have a standardised, 'official' fuel consumption and emissions test cycle, along the lines of the one used for cars and vans. Instead, bus manufacturers and such operators as TfL are able to compare like with like by running vehicles on the so-called Route 159 test at Millbrook Proving Ground. This test gives a guide to in-service consumption and allows useful fine tuning prior to commercial running. 'We normally expect a 20 per cent degradation from the standard test at Millbrook,' explains Hampson-Ghani, 'but we're getting more – though we are still better than the standard hybrid buses.'

Under the microscope are all the bus's key systems, including the lighting and the air-cooling. Many of the upgrades to the bus so far have been in the area of software, while a new and more efficient drive motor, a full 70 kilograms (154 lb) lighter, will soon be installed. TfL and Wrightbus operate a so-called gainshare scheme, whereby the two organisations share the benefit of any modifications that reduce costs or improve performance. Some of the bus's teething troubles, such as uncomfortably high temperatures on the upper deck in warm weather, gained widespread publicity. Yet, says Hampson-Ghani, very little has needed to be changed in terms of the bus's engineering, and customer satisfaction levels are very high.

During the conception phase for the New Routemaster, the engineers and designers were fully aware that tailoring the bus's specifications to London's requirements might reduce the chances of selling the vehicle to other cities or countries. However, David Barnett, now product director at Wrightbus and the man responsible for supervising the whole programme, believes that just because the

bus has been designed as a vehicle for London does not mean that it cannot be used outside London. 'With its open rear platform, it is perhaps questionable for cities without a history of the Routemaster', he advises. 'It's a different way of working – it's unique, eye-catching, and not a one-size-fits-all [solution]. It could be suitable for Edinburgh, say, and could be rolled out to other cities with TfL's blessing.'

TfL, which holds the intellectual property rights to almost every aspect of the design, as well as its overall look and feel, stands to gain financially from additional sales of the bus. Questioned as to whether London would be prepared to let other cities have the New Routemaster, Boris Johnson was extremely bullish: 'Of course. I'm sure Transport for London, Wrightbus and Thomas Heatherwick would be delighted to lend their expertise to any city that was looking to refresh its fleet of buses. In fact, we're already doing that. The New Routemaster has been on a globetrotting tour of such key markets as the United States and China as part of the "Great" campaign, which promotes London and the UK to the rest of the world [see pages 140–41]. The reception the bus got in Hong Kong, for example, was staggering. People stood agog, rooted to the street in amazement. I said while I was there that one of the advantages of the new bus is that it is the cleanest, greenest hybrid bus in the world. For such cities as Hong Kong and Beijing that are grappling with the challenges of air pollution, it would be the absolute perfect thing.'

Tempting though the prospect of global sales may be, the bus's engineers are more cautious because of the technical challenges involved. Surprisingly, however, it is local environmental regulations and the prevailing climate that pose the biggest hurdles, rather than the switch to left-hand drive for markets that drive on the right.

Creating a mirror-image bus is relatively straightforward, says Barnett. The design can simply be reversed – with the engine moving to the left-hand side, for instance – and new moulds and tooling would have to be made for many of the exterior body parts. The biggest challenge would be to adapt the hybrid driveline for use in a new environment, especially such hot climates as Hong Kong or Las Vegas. Currently, the energy usage on the bus in London is such that 50 per cent goes towards propulsion, while the remainder is used by such systems as power steering, air conditioning, lights and CCTV. Moving to a hotter climate would significantly increase the energy demanded by the air conditioning or cooling. In London, for example, the AC system is rated at approximately 12 kW, whereas Wrightbus's StreetCar model for Las Vegas requires 56 kW. Using the bus in such climates would clearly demand significant and costly changes to the powertrain. For his part, Barnett plays down the issue of export enquiries, saying that Wrightbus is currently focusing on fulfilling the 600-bus order from TfL.

Turning the Tables

As project manager for the New Routemaster, David Hampson-Ghani is understandably confident about the prospects opened up by the bus's design: 'We fully expect this bus to be a platform for technology that we have evolved or developed as a consequence of the project. We see it as a step change for the industry, something others will be forced to follow. It's a change that the manufacturers might by themselves have brought in only slowly, maybe taking ten years to implement.' In other words, says Hampson-Ghani, the project has successfully turned the tables in the bus industry. 'Instead of it being an industry-led market,' he explains, 'it's become more customer-led. We've told the manufacturers what bus we want, how we're going to design it, listed

ON MY RADAR | Una Stubbs's cultural highlights

Una Stubbs, 76, began her career as a dancer. She landed her first major acting job in Cliff Richard's 1963 film *Summer Holiday*, following that with the role of Rita in the sitcom *Till Death Do Us Part*. Later she played Aunt Sally in *Worzel Gummidge*, and captained a team on the gameshow *Give Us a Clue*. Recently she was part of the original cast of *The Curious Incident of the Dog in the Night-Time* at the National Theatre and will reprise her role as Mrs Hudson in *Sherlock*, which returns on Wednesday.
Leah Harper

Architecture

Thomas Heatherwick
He has come up with wonderful things such as the Olympic cauldron and the double-decker bus (the "new Routemaster") which you see bowling through London. When I'm standing at the bus stop, I always think: "Oh good, it's a Heatherwick."

Gardens

London's ga
There are m
squares in m
in any other
You can go a
a bench and
gorgeous it i
don't have to
weeding. Th
to where I liv
trees. What
seen over th

the clever things we want in it, and how it's going to look great. We are the biggest bus buyer in the UK, and perhaps other bus manufacturers will soon think they should begin to compete too.' According to Hampson-Ghani, however, the real benefits will lie in the more widespread application of the new technology, which he expects to happen 'by osmosis', rather than by regulation forced on the industry. On a more aesthetic level, and accepting Stuart Wood's assertion that the London bus is 'a cultural brand, not just a means of generating fares', the New Routemaster has demonstrated very successfully the benefits of knowing when to be cautious and when to be daring. 'We knew that when there were 600 of these on the streets,' says Wood, 'if we could make a small finessing of each one, there would be a large overall impact. We also knew that if we created a distinctive theme, these buses would have a presence. And that was a serious part of our brief – for the bus to have presence.'

Although the early signs indicate very strong customer acceptance of and high levels of public interest in the new design, it would be premature at this stage to grant the New Routemaster the iconic status of its predecessor, let alone to anticipate a fifty-year active service life. But two things have already been clearly established, perhaps signalling a fruitful way forward for the bus industry: individualised design is back on the menu, and so-called soft values – how people think and feel when they board a bus – are beginning to matter much more. 'We're dealing with the iPad generation here', says Hampson-Ghani. 'We're dealing with people who expect good design, and they see it on the new bus. There's very little vandalism, and we think it's possibly because people respect its holistic design – it's more Boeing than bus.' London is indeed special, asserts Mike Weston: 'Half of all the bus journeys in England take place in London. So it's not illogical to have a special design.'

These were precisely the arguments put forward in the 1950s when the original Routemaster was being developed. Its twenty-first-century protégé is already a major critical

English actress Una Stubbs lists the New Routemaster among her cultural highlights for a feature in *The Observer* ('On My Radar', 29 December 2013). 'When I'm standing at the bus stop,' she explains, 'I always think, "Oh good, it's a Heatherwick".'

The Best of British Manufacturing

Since becoming Mayor of London in 2008, Boris Johnson has been a tireless champion of London's individualism, and of the New Routemaster project in particular.

'London is the home of iconic design: our red post boxes and black taxis are recognisable around the world. The same was the case for the legendary red Routemaster bus, which did a sterling job on the streets of our capital for fifty-one years, and was loved by Londoners and visitors alike.

'Now – with the new bus – we've created a machine that is bang up to date with the latest green technology, as well as paying homage to the beautiful Routemaster design, showcasing the very best of British manufacturing. Not only that, but we are also creating jobs across the UK.

'The buses are built in Antrim, the engines come from Darlington, the seats are made in Telford, the destination signs are from Manchester, the seat moquette is made in Huddersfield, the ramps are from Hoddesdon and the Treadmaster flooring from Liskeard.'

and popular success in London, and other cities are showing strong interest, demonstrating the powerful appeal of a bus tailor-made to suit its customers. London is acknowledged as the design capital of the world, observes Sir Peter Hendy, and London Transport and its successor bodies have always been at the leading edge of contemporary design – be it in terms of vehicles, architecture or graphics. 'I care about design as much as Frank Pick [the acclaimed architect of London Transport's corporate identity in the interwar period] did', says Hendy. 'I see the New Routemaster as a return to London Transport's core design values. With it, we are replicating the design excellence this organisation has always been famous for.'

Some might argue that today's ever-tightening environmental standards make it unlikely that the New Routemaster will match its mentor's straight half-century in service. Yet TfL is already operating zero-emission electric and hydrogen fuel cell-powered buses in London, and the New Routemaster's technical template includes the flexibility to accommodate other forms of power. It could therefore prove unwise, as some have done, to bet against this stylish new bus becoming just as much of a long-term London landmark as its illustrious predecessor.

London Mayor Boris Johnson poses for photographers at the top of the staircase as the New Routemaster is first launched in the capital.

Technical Specifications

Wrightbus New Routemaster

Manufacturer	Wrightbus, Ballymena, Northern Ireland
Entry into service	2012
Number built	237 (as of May 2014)
Number ordered	600 (TfL only)
Cost per unit	£354,000
Passenger capacity upper deck	40 seats
lower deck	22 seats (includes 4 priority, 6 preferential); 1 wheelchair passenger, 25 standees

Dimensions and weights

Overall length	11,232 mm (442.2 in.)
Overall height	4,420 mm (174 in.)
Maximum width	2,520 mm (99.2 in.)
Wheelbase	6,000 mm (236.2 in.)
Step height (at ride height)	315 mm (12.4 in.), front two doors 335 mm (13.2 in.), rear platform
Step height (at kneel)	270 mm (10.6 in.), front two doors 335 mm (13.2 in.), rear platform
Interior headroom	1,810 mm (71.3 in.), upper deck 2,070 mm (81.5 in.), lower deck
Unladen weight	12,000 kg (26,455 lb)
Diesel fuel tank	200 litres (40 gallons)

Materials and finishes

Chassis	Rectangular hollow section steel (RHS) tube and channel sections
Body framework (central)	Aluminium castings, forgings and extrusions
Body framework (front)	Bolted and welded steel, aluminium sections
Body structure (rear)	Self-supporting composite structure bolted to main body and chassis
Body (roof)	Aluminium framework with full-length cantrails; single piece bonded aluminium roof panel with break-glass emergency escape panel
Interfloor	Aluminium extrusions, castings, forgings
Lower-deck floor	Step-free, composite board, plywood
Wheelarches	GRP, reinforced at stress points
Upper-deck floor	Plywood
Paint	Body: red; roof: white; wheels: Indian red

Powertrain

Configuration	Series hybrid
Engine	Cummins ISBe 4.5-litre four-cylinder diesel
Outputs	136 kW (182 hp), 700 Nm (516 lb ft)
After-treatment	Selective catalyst reduction (SCR) and diesel oxidation catalyst (DOC)
Emissions standard	Euro V EEV (Euro VI under development)
Generator	Siemens 180 kW
Drive motor	Siemens permanent magnet, 130 kW (174 hp), 1500 Nm (1,105 lb ft)
Battery	Lithium ion phosphate, 557V, liquid-cooled
Power inverters	Siemens-ELFA 2, 4-phase mono, liquid-cooled
DC–DC converter	600-24V, 300A, water-cooled
Air compressor	Independent, liquid-cooled, with integrated motor/inverter drive unit
Power steering	Independent, liquid-cooled, with integrated motor/inverter drive
Air-conditioning compressor	Belt-driven off engine

Chassis

Manufacturer	Wrightbus
Type	Low floor, hybrid, double-decker
Layout	Rear engine, inline right-hand side; rear-wheel drive
Front suspension	Independent, RL75 EC
Rear axle	AV 132
Suspension	Pneumatic, with rolling-type bellows
Kneeling	Complete nearside kneel
Service brake	Disc brakes to both axles; ABS and electronic control system with pneumatic back-up
Parking brake	Spring-loaded brake cylinders on rear axle

X-Type & B-Type

Manufacturer(s)	LGOC
Years manufactured	1909–10
Number built	60 (X-Type); > 3,000 (B-Type)
Passengers	34
Length	7 m (23 ft 2 in.)
Fuel	Petrol
Power	21–30 kW (28–40 hp)
Transmission	3-speed
Braking	Drums

K-Type

Manufacturer(s)	AEC (chassis); LGOC (bodywork)
Years manufactured	1919–21
Number built	1,132
Passengers	46
Length	6.9 m (22 ft 8 in.)
Engine	AEC 4-cylinder, 4.4-litre
Fuel	Petrol
Power	22 kW (30 hp)
Transmission	3-speed chain gear
Braking	Drums

NS-Type

Manufacturer(s)	AEC (chassis), LGOC (bodywork)
Years manufactured	1922–28
Number built	2,385
Passengers	52
Length	7.9 m (26 ft)
Engine	AEC 4-cylinder, 5.1-litre
Fuel	Petrol
Power	26/43 kW (35/57 hp)
Transmission	3-speed chain gear

LT

Manufacturer(s)	AEC, LGOC (chassis); LGOC, Short Bros. (bodywork)
Years manufactured	1929–32
Number built	1,227
Passengers	60
Length	8.2 m (26 ft 9 in.)
Engine	AEC 6-cylinder, 7.4-litre; 8.8-litre (diesel)
Fuel	Petrol, later diesel
Power	97 kW (130 hp)
Transmission	AEC 4-speed non-synchro or Daimler pre-selector
Braking	Servo, drums

ST/STL

Manufacturer(s)	AEC (chassis); LGOC, Short Bros. (bodywork)
Years manufactured	1929–32 (ST); 1932–39 (STL)
Number built	1,138 (ST); 2,659 (STL)
Passengers	49 (ST); 60 (STL)
Length	7.6 m (25 ft) (ST); 7.8 m (25 ft 5 in.) (STL)
Engine	AEC 6-cylinder, 6.1-litre (ST); 7.7-litre diesel (STL)
Fuel	Petrol (ST); diesel (STL)
Power	71 kW (95 hp)
Transmission	AEC 4-speed non-synchro
Braking	Servo, drums

RT

Manufacturer(s)	AEC (chassis); LT Chiswick (bodywork)
Years manufactured	1939–54
Number built	7,000
Passengers	56
Length	7.9 m (26 ft)
Engine	AEC 6-cylinder, 9.6-litre
Fuel	Diesel
Power	75 kW (100 hp)
Transmission	AEC 4-speed pre-selector, air operated
Braking	Air-pressure operated

Routemaster (RM)

Manufacturer(s)	AEC (chassis); Park Royal Vehicles (bodywork)
Years manufactured	1959–68
Number built	2,760
Passengers	64–72
Length	8.4 m (27 ft 6 in.) (RM); 9.1 m (29 ft 10 in.) (RML)
Engine	AEC 6-cylinder, 9.6-litre
Fuel	Diesel
Power	86 kW (115 hp)
Transmission	AEC 4-speed electro-pneumatic automatic
Steering	Power-assisted
Braking	Hydraulic power-assisted

Daimler Fleetline (DMS)

Manufacturer(s)	Daimler (chassis); PRV, MCW (bodywork)
Years manufactured	1969–76
Number built	2,646
Passengers	72
Length	9.3 m (30 ft 6 in.)
Engine	Gardner 6-cylinder, 10.5-litre
Fuel	Diesel
Power	127 kW (170 hp)
Transmission	Air-operated 4-speed automatic
Steering	Power-assisted
Braking	Air-pressure operated

MCW Metrobus (M)

Manufacturer(s)	Metropolitan (chassis)
Years manufactured	1980 onwards
Number built	1,440 (for LT)
Passengers	75
Length	9.5 m (31 ft 4 in.)
Engine	Gardner 6-cylinder
Fuel	Diesel
Power	127 kW (170 hp)
Transmission	Voith automatic with retarder
Steering	ZF assisted
Braking	Power

Wrightbus Eclipse Gemini 2

Manufacturer(s)	Volvo (chassis); Wrightbus (bodywork)
Years manufactured	2009 onwards
Passengers	62 (91 including standees)
Length	10.4 m (34 ft 2 in.)
Engine	Volvo D9B 6-cylinder
Fuel	Diesel
Power	194 kW (260 hp)
Transmission	ZF 6-speed automatic; retarder

Leyland Titan (T)

Manufacturer(s)	Leyland (chassis); PRV (bodywork)
Years manufactured	1978–84
Number built	1,125 (for LT)
Passengers	68
Length	9.5 m (31 ft 4 in.)
Engine	Gardner 6 LXB
Fuel	Diesel
Power	132 kW (177 hp)
Transmission	5-speed automatic
Steering	Powered rack-and-pinion
Braking	Hydraulically assisted

Dennis Trident & Enviro 400H

Manufacturer(s)	Alexander Dennis (chassis); Plaxton, Optare
Years manufactured	1997 onwards
Passengers	61–78
Length	10.2 m (33 ft 6 in.) – 11.4 m (37 ft 4 in.)
Engine	Cummins 4-cylinder, 4.5-litres (hybrid)
Fuel	Diesel
Power	138 kW (185 hp)
Transmission	BAE Systems HybriDrive
Steering	ZF power-assisted
Braking	Air-operated discs, ABS

Wrightbus Pulsar 2

Manufacturer(s)	VDL (chassis); Wrightbus (bodywork)
Years manufactured	2009 onwards
Number built	8 for London
Passengers	28 (58 including standees)
Length	11.9 m (39 ft)
Engine	Ballard fuel cell electric hybrid
Fuel	Hydrogen
Power	75 kW (100 hp)

Sources

Books

Ken Carr (ed.), *The London Bus Guide*, 3rd edn, Visions International Entertainment Ltd, 2013

Colin H. Curtis, *Buses of London: A Brief Historical Review*, London Transport Publications, 1977

Ken Glazier, *London Bus File*, various volumes 1933–66, Capital Transport Publishing, 1995–98

John Reed, *London Buses: A Brief History*, Capital Transport Publishing, 2007

Peter Stephens *et al.*, *London Transport Museum Souvenir Brochure*, 1982

James Taylor, *The London Bus*, Shire Publications, 2012

Transport for London and Department for Transport Documents

DfT Annual Bus Statistical Tables and Bus Summary Statistics

DfT Annual Bus Statistics: England, 2013

DfT National Travel Surveys 9903, 9904

Boris Johnson, *2020 Vision: The Greatest City on Earth*, Greater London Authority, 2013

TfL budgets, 2013–14

TfL business plans, 2005–13

TfL factsheets and internal documents

TfL Travel in London reports 1–6, 2009–13

London Transport and Historical Reports

T.C. Barker and Michael Robbins, *A History of London Transport: Passenger Travel and the Development of the Metropolis, Vol. 2 – The Twentieth Century to 1970*, Allen & Unwin, 1974

London County Council, *Statistical Abstract for London, 1939–1948, Vol. XXXI*, LCC Publications, 1950

London Transport (and predecessor bodies), annual reports, various years

D.L. Munby, *Inland Transport Statistics, Great Britain, 1900–1970*, Clarendon Press, 1978

Fiona Poole (ed.), *House of Commons Research Paper 99/59: Buses*, House of Commons Library, 1999

Magazines, Journals and Newspapers

Autocar
Car
Commercial Motor Archive
The Evening Standard
The Financial Times
GQ
The Guardian
Metro

Websites

bbc.co.uk/news
boriswatch.co.uk
busandcoach.com
busandcoachbuyer.com
coachandbusweek.com
designweek.co.uk
gov.uk
heatherwick.com
leondaniels.blogspot.com
london.gov.uk
londonbusmuseum.com
londonist.com
ltmuseum.co.uk
route-one.net
standard.co.uk
tfl.gov.uk
theguardian.com
transportextra.com
20thcenturylondon.org.uk
wrightbus.com

Picture Credits

Key: l = left; r = right; t = top; b = bottom; c = centre

Arup: 75r; © Iwan Baan: 72–73, 84tr, 126–27; © Ian Bell: 16–17, 32l; FCO: 140tr, 140b, 141tl, 141tr; FCO/© Clipper Race. Photo: Howie: 141b; FCO/© Masha Maltsava: 140tl; © Harrison Photography: 147; © Nick Harvey 2010: 8; Heatherwick Studio: 76l, 76b–77b, 80, 81, 84tl, 84b, 85; Heatherwick Studio/Hayes Davidson: 87; © James O. Jenkins : 79, 86l, 122–23, 132t–133t, 132b, 133b, 151; London Transport Museum Photographic Collection © TfL: 14–15, 20, 21 (all except br), 22 (all except bottom row), 23, 26l, 26r, 27l, 27r, 28l, 28r, 29, 30 (all), 31l, 31r, 32r, 33l; © Peter Macdiarmid/Getty Images: 25l, 25r, 34l; © Dan Maskell: 104; © Reuters/Pawel Kopczynski: 75l; © TfL: 21br, 22 (bottom row), 33r, 40–41, 42, 43, 44–45, 47, 48–63 (all), 64–65, 66, 67, 68, 83tr, 86r, 114t, 114b, 115t, 115b, 142–43; © TfL/Andy Rudak Photography: 4; © TfL, Photo Paul Curtis: 128c, 128b, 129; © TfL, Photo Michael Garnett: jacket (front), 12, 34r, 35, 130t, 131 (all except tr), 145, 148; © TfL, Photo Thomas Riggs: 128t; © TfL, Photo Phil Starling: 130b, 131rt; © Gerard Whyman: 71; Wrightbus: jacket (back), 2, 6, 10, 83bl, 88–89, 90, 91, 92t , 92b, 93, 95, 96 (all), 97l, 97r, 98t, 98b, 99l, 99r, 100t, 100b, 103, 105, 106 (all), 107, 108 (all), 109 (all), 110, 111t, 111b, 112 (all), 113 (all), 116–17, 118 (all), 119t, 119b, 120–21, 124–25, 134 (all), 135, 136–37, 138–39, 152–53, 160

Index

Page numbers in *italic* refer to the illustrations.

Acknowledgements

As an author who has spent most of his journalistic life discussing the design and engineering of cars, light trucks and motorcycles, I freely confess that it has been a steep learning curve to hop aboard a bus and get up to speed with the very different preoccupations of the bus industry. The complexities of bus building, the relationship between chassis suppliers and body makers, and even such mysterious concepts as the 'Route 159' test – all were challenges I needed to overcome. It has been a fascinating ride, however, aided in no small measure by the energy and encouragement of many key figures within Transport for London; senior officials, including Leon Daniels, Julie Dixon, David Ellis, David Hampson-Ghani, Sir Peter Hendy, Dan Maskell and Mike Weston, have been wonderfully enthusiastic and cooperative, despite their busy schedules.

At the opposite end of the bus business my thanks go to the staff and drivers at Holloway bus garage for their insights into the day-to-day operation of the New Routemaster. I am also indebted to the support staff at the Mayor of London's office for successfully tracking down their boss to answer my many questions.

At the core of the story behind the New Routemaster project are the engineers and designers whose creative vision made the final product so remarkable. My special thanks therefore go to Stuart Wood at Heatherwick Studio, and to David Barnett, Paul Blair, Patrick Chapman, Neil Coulter and Sean McCartney at Wrightbus in Northern Ireland, all of whom put up with many hours of interrogation from me and answered each question with scrupulous patience.

On the historical side, the resources – especially the library – of the London Transport Museum in Covent Garden have been invaluable, as has the remarkable depth of knowledge of head librarian Caroline Warhurst, who guided me straight to the most useful volumes in the huge collection. And an element of more recent history has been added by my journalist colleague Hilton Holloway, who can justifiably claim to have been one of the sparks that set light to the whole New Routemaster discussion, back in 2007.

Finally, I would like to thank the team at Merrell Publishers: Hugh Merrell, for somehow persuading me to step up to this task, despite the near-impossible schedule; designer Nicola Bailey; and editor Mark Ralph, for once again putting up with my foibles and simplifying complicated sentences, and also for his zero-tolerance attitude to technical terms, forcing me to define them everywhere they crop up.

The publishers, Transport for London and the author would like to thank Martin S. Curtis for his invaluable contribution to the making of this book. Martin S. Curtis has been writing about the design, manufacture and operation of buses for more than five decades. He is currently Managing Director of Bath Bus Company, which became only the second operator – and the first outside London – to run a New Routemaster on one of its services.

First published 2014 by Merrell Publishers, London and New York

Merrell Publishers Limited
70 Cowcross Street
London EC1M 6EJ

merrellpublishers.com

in association with

Transport for London
Windsor House
42–50 Victoria Street
London SW1H 0TL

tfl.gov.uk

Text copyright © 2014 Merrell Publishers Limited, with the following exceptions: forewords, preface and introduction copyright © 2014 Transport for London
Illustrations copyright © 2014 the copyright holders; see page 157
Design and layout copyright © 2014 Merrell Publishers Limited

All rights reserved. No part of this publication may be reproduced, stored in a retrieval system or transmitted, in any form or by any means, electronic, mechanical, photocopying, recording or otherwise, without the prior written permission of the publishers.

British Library Cataloguing-in-Publication Data:
A catalogue record for this book is available from the British Library

ISBN 978-1-8589-4624-5

Produced by Merrell Publishers Limited
Designed by Nicola Bailey
Project-managed by Mark Ralph
Indexed by Hilary Bird

Printed and bound in Italy

The publishers have made every effort to trace and contact copyright holders of the material reproduced in this book. They will be happy to correct in subsequent editions any errors or omissions that are brought to their attention.

Page 4: The distinctive silhouette of the London double-decker has been exploited since the 1930s in London Transport's famous publicity posters. Now, true to that tradition, a stylised New Routemaster is portrayed in this Transport for London image against London landmarks both new and old.